Hugging Face Trans

I0007713

Build Advanced LLM's For Developers

Written by

Evan Walters

Table of Contents

Preface: Welcome to the Cutting Edge of Text Generation!

Hey there, fellow code wizard! Are you ready to **unlock the secret sauce of language with the power of Hugging Face Transformers and build jaw-dropping LLMs that will leave your peers speechless**? Buckle up, because this book is your passport to that mind-blowing reality!

Forget the days of clunky, robotic text generation. We're talking **next-level, human-quality language you can craft with just a few lines of code**. Imagine chatbots that hold captivating conversations, AI assistants that write you poetry on demand, or content creation tools that churn out marketing copy that converts like magic. **It's not science fiction anymore, it's the power you'll wield after diving into this book.**

Now, you might be thinking, "Transformers? LLMs? Sounds complex!" But fear not, my code-slinging friend. **Think of this book as your friendly neighborhood tour guide on this adventure.** We'll start with the basics, unraveling the magic behind Transformers and the Hugging Face ecosystem. Then, we'll **gradually crank up the intensity, teaching you how to fine-tune pre-trained models, craft your own LLM architectures, and deploy them into real-world applications.**

But this isn't just a dry technical manual. We'll keep things fun, peppering the journey with practical examples, code snippets you can experiment with, and even a dash of humor (because let's face it, staring at code all day can get a bit…well, code-y).

By the end of this book, you won't just understand LLMs, you'll be their master. You'll be **building language models that not only generate text, but understand it, respond to it, and even create something entirely new.** Sounds pretty darn cool, right?

*So, what are you waiting for? **Turn the page and let's embark on this exciting journey together. The future of language awaits, and you hold the key to unlocking its potential!***

Chapter 1: Dive into the Languageverse: Your NLP Adventure Begins!

Imagine being able to chat with a computer that truly understands you, not just responds with pre-programmed answers. Or think about automatically generating personalized marketing copy that converts like crazy. Sounds like something out of a sci-fi movie, right? Wrong! Welcome to the fascinating world of Natural Language Processing (NLP), where computers are learning to speak our language – and we're about to become their teachers!

But before we start coding magical language bots, let's demystify this whole NLP thing. Think of it as deciphering the secret code humans use to communicate. We analyze text, speech, and everything in between, helping computers understand the nuances of language, from grammar and syntax to sarcasm and sentiment. It's like teaching a baby to talk, but way cooler (and less drool-inducing, hopefully!).

1.1 What is NLP? Demystifying the World of Language Processing

Natural Language Processing (NLP) is a branch of artificial intelligence (AI) concerned with the interaction between computers and human language. In simpler terms, it's about teaching computers to understand and process language in a way that is meaningful to humans.

This goes far beyond basic tasks like keyword matching or spell checking. NLP encompasses a wide range of abilities, including:

- Understanding the meaning of text: Analyzing the context, sentiment, and intent behind words.
- Generating human-quality text: Creating coherent and grammatically correct sentences, even for complex topics.
- Translating languages: Accurately converting text from one language to another, preserving the nuances of meaning.
- Classifying text: Categorizing documents or sentences based on their content.
- Extracting information: Identifying key entities and relationships from text (e.g., people, places, dates).

While chatbots are a popular application of NLP, they represent just a small slice of its potential. NLP is used in various fields, including:

- Machine translation: Powering tools like Google Translate and enabling real-time communication across languages.
- Search engines: Understanding user queries and ranking relevant results.
- Social media analysis: Identifying trends and sentiment in online conversations.
- Voice assistants: Enabling devices like Siri and Alexa to understand and respond to spoken language.
- Content creation: Generating marketing copy, product descriptions, or even creative text formats like poems or code.

By understanding NLP, developers can unlock new possibilities for human-computer interaction and create intelligent systems that can truly understand and respond to our needs.

Key Terms:

- Natural Language Processing (NLP): The field of AI concerned with computer processing of human language.

- Machine translation: Automatically translating text from one language to another.
- Sentiment analysis: Determining the emotional tone of a text.
- Chatbot: A computer program that simulates conversation with human users.
- Voice assistant: A software program that understands and responds to spoken language commands.

I hope this explanation provides a clear and concise overview of NLP, suitable for both beginners and experienced developers. If you have any further questions or specific areas you'd like to explore deeper, feel free to ask!

1.2 Key tasks in NLP: It's Like Training Your Language-Learning Computer Pet

Just like we wouldn't expect a new puppy to understand our commands instantly, training computers to process language requires focused effort. NLP focuses on specific tasks to gradually build their language comprehension. Here are some key areas:

1. Text Classification: Imagine sorting a mountain of emails. NLP algorithms can do this automatically, classifying text based on its content. Is a tweet positive or negative? Is a document relevant to a specific topic? These are just a few examples of classification tasks.

2. Named Entity Recognition (NER): Ever wondered how search engines pinpoint specific information in your queries? NER is the key! It helps identify important entities within text, like people, organizations, locations, or dates. Think of it as underlining the crucial nouns in a sentence for the computer to understand.

3. Machine Translation: Bridging language barriers is a core NLP ambition. Machine translation systems use complex algorithms to accurately translate text from one language to another. This involves understanding the nuances of each language, making it a constantly evolving challenge.

4. Text Summarization: Information overload is real! NLP can condense lengthy texts into concise summaries, extracting key points and saving you precious time. Imagine summarizing a research paper or news article in just a few sentences – that's the power of summarization.

5. Question Answering: Remember chatbots answering your questions? NLP algorithms power this ability. They analyze information sources and formulate responses based on the context and intent of your question. This opens doors for intelligent search assistants and more natural human-computer interactions.

Beyond these, NLP delves into complex tasks like parsing sentence structure, identifying sarcasm, and even generating creative text formats. Each task requires specialized techniques and algorithms, contributing to the overall goal of empowering computers to truly understand and process human language.

Key Terms:

- Text Classification: Categorizing text based on its content.
- Named Entity Recognition (NER): Identifying important entities (people, locations, etc.) within text.
- Machine Translation: Automatically translating text from one language to another.
- Text Summarization: Condensing lengthy texts into concise summaries.
- Question Answering: Providing answers to questions based on given information.

Remember, NLP is a diverse field with a vast array of tasks and applications. Mastering these core areas forms the foundation for exploring further advancements and building impactful solutions with the power of language processing.

1.3 The Rise of Large Language Models (LLMs): Unleashing the Language Superheroes

Imagine an AI model that can write poetry, translate languages with nuance, and even answer your questions in an informative way. These aren't science fiction dreams anymore – they're the reality of Large Language Models (LLMs).

Think of LLMs as superpowered versions of traditional NLP models. Trained on massive datasets of text and code, they possess remarkable abilities:

- Generating human-quality text: Forget robotic outputs; LLMs can create natural-sounding text for various purposes, from writing product descriptions to crafting marketing copy.
- Exceptional translation: Going beyond basic word replacements, LLMs capture the subtleties of different languages, delivering accurate and nuanced translations.
- Question answering expertise: Equipped with vast knowledge, LLMs can answer your questions comprehensively, drawing insights from various sources and understanding the context behind your queries.
- Creative content generation: Unleash your imagination! LLMs can generate poems, code snippets, scripts, and even musical pieces, pushing the boundaries of creative expression with AI.

But how do these language superheroes work? Well, it's all thanks to complex architectures like Transformers, which we'll delve into in the next chapter. For now, understand that LLMs are constantly evolving, learning from the vast amounts of data they consume.

With such capabilities, LLMs are revolutionizing numerous fields:

- Personalization: Imagine chatbots that truly understand your needs and respond accordingly. LLMs can personalize user experiences, making interactions more natural and engaging.
- Content creation: Say goodbye to writer's block! LLMs can assist in content creation, generating ideas, drafting text, and even suggesting revisions.
- Search and information retrieval: Forget sifting through irrelevant results. LLMs can power smarter search engines that understand your intent and deliver the most relevant information.

The potential of LLMs is vast and constantly expanding. By understanding their capabilities and the underlying technology, you can unlock new possibilities for your own projects and contribute to the exciting future of language processing.

Key Terms:

- Large Language Models (LLMs): Highly powerful AI models trained on massive text and code datasets.
- Natural language processing (NLP): The field of AI concerned with computer processing of human language.
- Transformers: A specific type of neural network architecture commonly used in LLMs.

Remember, LLMs are just one piece of the NLP puzzle. By understanding the broader field and its various tasks, you'll be well-equipped to leverage the power of LLMs and explore their potential in your own endeavors.

Chapter 2: Transformers: Dive into the Magic Behind LLMs!

So, you're pumped about LLMs, right? But before we unleash their full potential, let's peek under the hood and explore the secret sauce: Transformers! Buckle up, because this isn't your average tech talk. We're going on an exciting journey to understand the architecture that powers these language superheroes.

2.1 Understanding the Transformer Architecture: Decoding the Engine Powering LLMs

At the heart of Large Language Models (LLMs) lies a revolutionary architecture called the Transformer. While the underlying mathematics might seem complex, grasping its core principles is crucial to understanding these powerful models. Fear not, for this section will navigate the key concepts in a clear and approachable way.

The Transformer's Power of Parallelism: Unlike traditional sequential models, Transformers process information in parallel. Imagine analyzing all the words in a sentence simultaneously, instead of one by one. This allows them to capture relationships between words across the entire sentence, leading to a deeper understanding of meaning.

Encoder-Decoder Magic: Transformers utilize two key components: encoders and decoders. The encoder acts like a language analyst, processing the input text (think of it as the raw ingredients) and generating a hidden representation that captures its meaning. The decoder, like a skilled chef, uses this hidden representation to create the output text (the final dish). This approach enables tasks like machine translation and conversation generation.

Attention Mechanism: The Spotlight on Relevance: But the true magic lies in the attention mechanism. Imagine each word in a sentence vying for attention. The attention mechanism acts like a spotlight, allocating more focus to relevant words based on their context and importance. This allows the model to prioritize crucial information, leading to more accurate and nuanced outputs.

Key Terms:

- Transformer: A neural network architecture used in LLMs, known for its parallel processing and attention mechanism.
- Encoder: Processes input text and generates a hidden representation of its meaning.
- Decoder: Uses the hidden representation from the encoder to generate the output text.
- Attention mechanism: Allocates focus to relevant parts of the input, improving the accuracy and nuance of the output.

By understanding these fundamental concepts, you gain a solid foundation for exploring Transformers further. Remember, the complexity lies in the underlying math, but the core principles are accessible and pave the way for exciting explorations in the world of LLMs. In the next chapter, we'll delve into the Hugging Face ecosystem, your gateway to building your own LLMs powered by these remarkable Transformers!

2.2 Encoder-Decoder Models: The Backbone of Sequence-to-Sequence Tasks

Now, let's shift our focus to encoder-decoder models, the workhorses behind tasks like machine translation and chatbot conversations. These models excel at handling sequence-to-sequence tasks, where they process one sequence of information (input) and generate another related sequence (output).

Understanding the Encoder-Decoder Dance:

- The Encoder: Imagine the encoder as a skilled listener. It reads the input sequence (e.g., a sentence in one language) and carefully analyzes the relationships between words. Its goal is to capture the essence of the meaning and condense it into a hidden representation. Think of this as summarizing the key points of the conversation in your head.
- The Decoder: Now comes the decoder, our language maestro. Taking the hidden representation from the encoder, it starts generating the output sequence (e.g., the translated sentence). But here's the twist – the decoder doesn't blindly create new words. It constantly consults the encoder's hidden representation, ensuring its output stays relevant and coherent. It's like referencing your notes while retelling a story, making sure you capture the gist while adding your own flair.

Beyond Translation: A Spectrum of Applications:

While machine translation is a popular example, encoder-decoder models have diverse applications:

- Chatbots: Imagine having a conversation with a virtual assistant who truly understands your questions and responds contextually. Encoder-decoder models power these interactions, analyzing your input and generating relevant responses.
- Text summarization: Need the key points of a long article without reading the whole thing? These models can condense lengthy texts into concise summaries, saving you precious time.
- Creative text generation: Unleash your imagination! Encoder-decoder models can be trained to generate poems, code snippets, scripts, and even musical pieces, pushing the boundaries of creative expression with AI.

Key Terms:

- Encoder-decoder model: A neural network architecture specifically designed for sequence-to-sequence tasks.
- Encoder: Processes the input sequence and generates a hidden representation of its meaning.
- Decoder: Uses the hidden representation from the encoder to generate the output sequence.
- Sequence-to-sequence task: A task where the input and output are both sequences of information (e.g., machine translation, text summarization).

By understanding the core principles of encoder-decoder models, you unlock a powerful tool for various NLP applications. As we delve deeper, remember that these models are just one piece of the puzzle. In the next chapter, we'll explore the Hugging Face ecosystem, where you'll discover how to leverage pre-trained models and tools to build your own LLMs!

2.3 Attention Mechanisms: The Secret Sauce of Understanding in Transformers

Remember the "spotlight" analogy from the previous chapter? It perfectly captures the essence of attention mechanisms, the game-changing feature within Transformers that truly sets them apart. Let's break down this crucial concept in a clear and understandable way.

Imagine a complex sentence with multiple clauses and nuances. Traditional models process each word sequentially, struggling to grasp the connections between distant elements. But Transformers, with their attention mechanisms, are different. Think of them as having multiple spotlights, each focusing on different parts of the sentence simultaneously.

Here's how it works:

1. Each word gets its own spotlight: The model assigns scores to every word pair, indicating their relevance to each other. Imagine each word vying for attention, with important ones receiving brighter spotlights.
2. Contextual understanding emerges: By focusing on relevant words, the model captures the meaning of the sentence more accurately. Words like pronouns or connecting phrases, often crucial for understanding, receive the spotlight they deserve.
3. Long-range dependencies are bridged: Attention mechanisms allow the model to connect elements far apart in the sentence. Think of a joke where the punchline relies on something mentioned earlier – attention ensures the model gets it!

Benefits of Attention Mechanisms:

- Improved accuracy: By focusing on relevant parts, the model generates more accurate outputs in tasks like translation or text summarization.
- Nuance and context: Attention allows the model to capture subtle meanings and context, leading to more natural and human-like outputs.
- Long-range understanding: The ability to connect distant elements is crucial for tasks like question answering or sarcasm detection, areas where attention shines.

Key Terms:

- Attention mechanism: A core feature in Transformers that assigns weights to word pairs, allowing the model to focus on relevant parts of the input for better understanding.
- Spotlight analogy: Used to illustrate how attention mechanisms focus on specific words based on their importance in the context.
- Long-range dependencies: Relationships between words that are far apart in a sentence, which attention mechanisms are especially adept at capturing.

By understanding attention mechanisms, you gain a deeper appreciation for the power of Transformers. Remember, this is just the beginning. In the next chapter, we'll explore the Hugging Face ecosystem, where you'll discover how to leverage pre-trained models with attention mechanisms to build your own LLMs!

Chapter 3: The Hugging Face Ecosystem: Your LLM Playground Awaits!

Ready to dive into the world of building your own LLMs? Buckle up, because we're about to explore the Hugging Face ecosystem, your one-stop shop for everything LLM-related! Think of it as your personal gateway to unleashing the power of language models and creating something truly extraordinary.

3.1 Unveiling the Hugging Face Library: Your Gateway to LLM Exploration

Excited to embark on your LLM development journey? Look no further than the Hugging Face library, your essential toolkit for navigating this realm. Imagine an open-source treasure trove specifically designed for NLP tasks, offering a wealth of resources to empower your LLM creations.

More Than Just Code: While the library itself boasts an impressive collection of tools and functionalities, the Hugging Face ecosystem extends far beyond mere lines of code. It fosters a vibrant community of developers and researchers, united by their passion for NLP and LLMs. This means you'll have access to a treasure trove of knowledge, tutorials, and support throughout your exploration.

Pre-trained Models: The Powerhouse of Potential:

Now, let's talk about the real stars of the show: pre-trained models. Think of them as language experts trained on massive datasets of text and code, ready to be fine-tuned for your specific needs. Imagine having access to a multilingual master capable of understanding diverse writing styles and even humor – that's the potential pre-trained models unlock.

The Hugging Face Hub is your one-stop shop for discovering these gems. You'll find models adept at various tasks, from translation and text summarization to question answering and creative text generation. It's like having a buffet of pre-trained language skills, waiting to be incorporated and adapted to your unique project.

Datasets: The Fuel for Learning: But remember, building exceptional LLMs requires not just the models themselves, but also the data they learn from. Enter Hugging Face Datasets, a constantly expanding collection of high-quality datasets covering diverse topics and languages. These datasets provide the essential fuel for your pre-trained models, enabling them to truly excel.

Key Terms:

- Hugging Face library: An open-source library specifically designed for NLP tasks, providing tools and resources for LLM development.
- Pre-trained models: LLM models trained on massive datasets, ready to be fine-tuned for specific tasks.
- Hugging Face Hub: A platform for discovering and sharing pre-trained models and datasets.
- Hugging Face Datasets: A collection of high-quality datasets for various NLP tasks.

By understanding these core elements, you're well-equipped to delve deeper into the Hugging Face ecosystem. In the next chapter, we'll shift gears to the practical side, guiding you through building your first LLM, fine-tuning pre-trained models, and harnessing the power of the community. Are you ready to unlock the true potential of language with Hugging Face? Turn the page, and let's get started!

3.2 Pre-trained Models & Datasets: The Bedrock of LLM Success

Building effective LLMs requires potent ingredients, and the Hugging Face ecosystem provides two crucial ones: pre-trained models and datasets. Let's explore how these elements act as the foundation for your LLM endeavors.

Pre-trained Models: Supercharged Language Experts:

Imagine having access to a team of language experts, each trained on vast amounts of text and code. That's essentially what pre-trained models offer. These models, already well-versed in various language tasks, become the starting point for your LLM journey.

Think of them as language athletes who have undergone rigorous training. You don't need to teach them the basics of grammar or vocabulary – they're ready to tackle specific tasks with fine-tuning. The Hugging Face Hub overflows with these pre-trained models, each specializing in different areas like:

- Machine translation: Seamlessly convert text from one language to another.
- Text summarization: Condense lengthy articles into concise summaries.
- Question answering: Get insightful answers to your queries.

- Creative text generation: Unleash your imagination with poems, code, scripts, and more.

Choosing the right pre-trained model is crucial. Consider the specific task you want your LLM to perform and select a model trained on similar data. Remember, you're not starting from scratch – you're leveraging the power of pre-existing knowledge!

Datasets: The Fuel for Learning and Growth:

Just like any expert, pre-trained models need continuous learning to improve. This is where datasets come in. Think of them as the diverse learning materials that feed your LLM's knowledge base. The Hugging Face Datasets collection offers a wealth of high-quality datasets covering various topics and languages.

Imagine feeding your LLM a rich diet of text data related to your specific task. For example, if you're building a medical chatbot, providing medical dialogue datasets helps the LLM understand the nuances of the domain. The more relevant and diverse the data, the better your LLM will learn and perform.

Key Terms:

- Pre-trained model: A pre-trained neural network with existing knowledge in a specific language task, ready for fine-tuning.
- Fine-tuning: Adapting a pre-trained model to a specific task by training it on a new dataset.
- Hugging Face Hub: A platform for discovering and sharing pre-trained models and datasets.
- Hugging Face Datasets: A collection of high-quality datasets for various NLP tasks.

By understanding these building blocks, you're now prepared to delve deeper into the practical aspects of LLM development. In the next chapter, we'll guide you through building your first LLM, fine-tuning pre-trained models, and harnessing the power of the Hugging Face community. Are you ready to bring your LLM vision to life? Turn the page, and let's get building!

3.3 Community & Resources: Your Network for LLM Success

Remember, the journey of building exceptional LLMs isn't a solitary one. The Hugging Face ecosystem thrives on a vibrant community of developers, researchers, and enthusiasts, all united by their passion for language models. This supportive network provides invaluable resources and fosters collaborative learning, propelling you forward in your LLM development journey.

Learning Together:

- Forum: Engage in active discussions, ask questions, and share your experiences with fellow LLM builders. Get insights from diverse perspectives and learn from their successes and challenges.
- Tutorials & Documentation: Access a wealth of comprehensive tutorials and detailed documentation, covering everything from basic concepts to advanced techniques. Master new skills and stay up-to-date with the latest advancements in the field.
- Blogs & Articles: Stay informed by reading insightful blog posts and articles written by community experts. Gain valuable knowledge and discover innovative approaches to LLM development.

Growing Together:

- Contribute to Open Source: Give back to the community by contributing to open-source projects within the Hugging Face ecosystem. Share your code, datasets, and knowledge, enriching the ecosystem for everyone.
- Attend Events & Meetups: Participate in online and offline events organized by the Hugging Face community. Connect with fellow enthusiasts, network with potential collaborators, and learn from inspiring talks and workshops.
- Share Your Work: Showcase your LLM creations with the community! Present your projects, discuss their capabilities, and receive valuable feedback to further refine your work.

Key Terms:

- Community: The network of developers, researchers, and enthusiasts within the Hugging Face ecosystem, collaborating and supporting each other in LLM development.
- Collaborative learning: The process of acquiring knowledge and skills through interaction and knowledge sharing within the community.
- Open-source contribution: Sharing your code, datasets, and knowledge with the community to benefit the collective development of LLMs.

By actively engaging with the Hugging Face community, you unlock a treasure trove of resources, gain invaluable support, and contribute to the collective advancement of LLM technology. Remember, collaboration is key - together, we can push the boundaries of what's possible with language models!

In the next chapter, we'll delve into the practical aspects of using the Hugging Face ecosystem. We'll guide you through building your first LLM, fine-tuning pre-trained models, and leveraging the power of the community. Are you ready to unleash your LLM potential? Turn the page, and let's get started!

Chapter 4: Fine-tuning the Language Superpower: Unleashing Your LLM's Potential!

So you've got the pre-trained LLM muscles, now it's time to fine-tune them into a lean, mean language machine! In this chapter, we'll delve into the exciting world of fine-tuning, where you take a pre-trained model and mold it into a master of your specific task. Buckle up, because we're about to unlock the true potential of your LLM!

4.1 Matchmaker, Matchmaker: Selecting the Perfect Model and Dataset for Your LLM

Remember that pre-trained LLM is like a versatile athlete – they possess general language skills, but to excel in a specific sport (your task), they need targeted training. This chapter guides you through selecting the right model and dataset, the crucial ingredients for fine-tuning success.

Choosing the Champion: The Right Pre-trained Model

Imagine selecting the perfect starting pitcher for your baseball team. Different models have varying strengths and weaknesses. Consider these factors when choosing yours:

- Task Alignment: Is the model trained on a similar task? For instance, for sentiment analysis, a model pre-trained on large amounts of text with sentiment labels would be ideal.
- Performance Benchmarks: Check the model's performance on standard benchmarks related to your task. Higher scores often indicate better suitability.
- Available Resources: Consider your computational resources. Some models are lightweight, while others demand significant processing power. Choose one that aligns with your capabilities.

Remember, the chosen model sets the foundation for your LLM's capabilities. Select wisely, and you'll be well on your way to building a champion in your chosen domain.

Fueling the Journey: The Perfect Dataset for Fine-tuning

Now, think of the dataset as the high-quality training regimen for your athlete. It should:

- Be Relevant: Does the content align with your task? For building a medical chatbot, a dataset of medical dialogues would be most relevant.
- Be Diverse: Expose your LLM to various aspects of the task and different writing styles. Diversity fostersgeneralizability.
- Be High-Quality: Ensure the data is accurate, free of biases, and well-formatted. Remember, "garbage in, garbage out" applies to LLMs as well.

By carefully selecting a dataset that aligns with your task and adheres to these quality standards, you provide the fuel for your LLM to truly excel.

Key Terms:

- Pre-trained model: A neural network with existing knowledge in a general language domain, ready for fine-tuning for specific tasks.
- Fine-tuning: Adapting a pre-trained model to a specific task by training it on a new dataset.
- Task alignment: Choosing a model pre-trained on a task similar to yours for better fine-tuning effectiveness.
- Performance benchmarks: Standardized tests or metrics used to evaluate a model's performance on a specific task.
- Dataset: A collection of labeled data used to train machine learning models.

With a solid understanding of model and dataset selection, you're ready to delve into the art of fine-tuning in the next chapter. Remember, the right tools are the foundation for crafting your LLM masterpiece!

4.2 Fine-tuning Techniques: Sculpting Your LLM into a Masterpiece

Now that you've chosen your champion model and their training regimen (dataset), it's time to unleash the art of fine-tuning. Think of it like meticulously sculpting a masterpiece – applying targeted techniques to transform your LLM into a master of your specific task. Let's explore some key approaches:

1. Transfer Learning: Building on Strong Foundations:

Imagine training a new athlete who already possesses strong fundamentals. That's the essence of transfer learning. Leverage the pre-trained model's existing knowledge of language while focusing on your specific task. It's like teaching your LLM the nuances of your domain without erasing its general language understanding.

2. Freezing Layers: Protecting Valuable Knowledge:

Certain layers within the pre-trained model hold vital general language knowledge. Freezing these layers during fine-tuning ensures you don't accidentally erase this valuable information while adapting the model to your specific task. Imagine carefully preserving the core techniques of your athlete while refining them for a new sport.

3. Regularization Techniques: Preventing Overfitting and Boosting Generalizability:

Think of overfitting as your athlete becoming too focused on one specific training technique, hindering their performance in real-world scenarios. Regularization techniques like dropout or weight decay help prevent this by introducing some randomness during training, encouraging the LLM to learn more generalizable patterns.

4. Hyperparameter Tuning: Finding the Perfect Balance:

Just like finding the optimal training regimen for an athlete, hyperparameter tuning involves adjusting various settings within the fine-tuning process to achieve the best possible performance. Experiment with different learning rates, batch sizes, and optimizers to identify the sweet spot for your LLM.

5. Early Stopping: Knowing When to Say Enough:

Overtraining can be detrimental, just like pushing an athlete beyond their limits. Early stopping monitors the LLM's performance on a validation set and halts training when further improvement ceases, preventing overfitting and wasted resources.

Remember, fine-tuning is an iterative process. Experiment with different techniques, analyze results, and refine your approach to sculpt your LLM into a true champion.

Key Terms:

- Fine-tuning: Adapting a pre-trained model to a specific task by training it on a new dataset.
- Transfer learning: Leveraging the knowledge of a pre-trained model for a new task while focusing on specific adaptations.
- Freezing layers: Preventing specific layers in a pre-trained model from being updated during fine-tuning to preserve their general language knowledge.
- Regularization techniques: Methods to prevent overfitting and improve the generalizability of a model.
- Hyperparameter tuning: Adjusting settings within the fine-tuning process to optimize performance.
- Early stopping: Halting training when further improvement on a validation set ceases to prevent overfitting.

By mastering these techniques, you unlock the true potential of fine-tuning, transforming your LLM from a promising athlete into a dominant force in your chosen domain. In the next chapter, we'll delve into the exciting world of real-world LLM applications, showcasing how others have applied these techniques to create groundbreaking solutions. Get ready to be inspired!

4.3 Evaluating and Interpreting Results: Unveiling the Victories (and Learning Opportunities) of Your LLM

You've meticulously fine-tuned your LLM, but how do you know it's performing at its peak? Enter the crucial stage of evaluation and interpretation, where you analyze the results and decipher your LLM's strengths and weaknesses. Think of it like studying the scorecard after a competition – it reveals areas for celebration and opportunities for growth.

Choosing the Right Metrics: Beyond the Generic Scoreboard

Don't fall into the trap of generic metrics! Select task-specific metrics that truly reflect your LLM's success. For example, BLEU score measures the quality of machine translation, while ROUGE score assesses text summarization effectiveness. Choose metrics that align with your goals and provide meaningful insights.

Analyzing Outputs: Going Beyond the Numbers

Metrics offer valuable guidance, but don't neglect the actual outputs your LLM generates. Scrutinize them closely:

- Are they relevant to the task at hand?
- Do they exhibit coherence and grammatical correctness?
- Can you identify patterns in errors or successes?

Analyze both positive and negative outputs to gain deeper understanding of your LLM's capabilities and limitations.

Iterate and Refine: The Journey Continues

Remember, evaluation is an ongoing process, not a one-time event. Use your findings to:

- Refine your fine-tuning approach: Experiment with different techniques, hyperparameters, or datasets based on your observations.
- Address specific weaknesses: If your LLM struggles with a certain type of input, curate additional training data or adjust your fine-tuning strategy.
- Celebrate successes: Acknowledge and appreciate your LLM's achievements! This motivates further refinement and experimentation.

Key Terms:

- Evaluation: Assessing the performance of your LLM on a specific task.
- Interpretation: Analyzing the results of evaluation to understand your LLM's strengths and weaknesses.
- Task-specific metrics: Metrics designed to evaluate the performance of an LLM on a particular task (e.g., BLEU score for translation, ROUGE score for summarization).
- Iterative process: The ongoing cycle of evaluating, interpreting, and refining your LLM's performance.

By adopting a data-driven and analytical approach to evaluation and interpretation, you transform your LLM from a promising contender into a true champion, continuously learning and evolving to excel in your chosen domain. In the next chapter, we'll explore inspiring real-world examples of how others have leveraged these techniques to create groundbreaking LLM applications. Prepare to be amazed by the possibilities!

Chapter 5: Advanced Fine-tuning: Unleashing the LLM Beast Within!

Ready to take your LLM game to the next level? Buckle up, language enthusiasts, because this chapter dives into the advanced fine-tuning techniques that'll push your models beyond their perceived limits! Think of it as equipping your LLM with performance-enhancing gear, ready to tackle even the most challenging tasks.

5.1 Multi-tasking Mastery: Learning Like a Language Ninja

Imagine training your athlete in multiple sports simultaneously, each enhancing their overall skills and performance. That's the essence of multi-task learning, a powerful technique for unlocking the true potential of your LLMs. Let's delve into this approach and discover how it empowers your language models to become true language ninjas!

The Power of Multi-tasking:

- Boost Performance: By training on multiple related tasks concurrently, your LLM gains a deeper understanding of language nuances and representations. This cross-pollination of knowledge often leads to improved performance on each individual task. Think of your athlete mastering footwork drills that benefit both their soccer and basketball games.
- Data Efficiency: Training multiple tasks simultaneously leverages shared knowledge, potentially reducing the need for massive datasets specific to each task. This is

particularly beneficial when data is scarce or acquiring it is expensive.
- Real-World Ready: The LLM exposed to diverse language applications through multi-tasking learns more adaptable and generalizable representations. This equips them to handle new situations and challenges with greater flexibility, just like a true language ninja!

Key Concepts:

- Multi-task learning: Training an LLM on multiple related tasks simultaneously to improve performance and knowledge transfer.
- Shared representations: The underlying patterns and concepts learned from one task that can be applied to other tasks.
- Generalizability: The ability of an LLM to adapt its knowledge and skills to new and unseen situations.

Examples of Multi-tasking:

- Training a chatbot to handle both customer service inquiries and product recommendations.
- Teaching a text summarization model to summarize different types of documents, like news articles and research papers.
- Fine-tuning a machine translation model for multiple languages simultaneously.

Remember: While multi-tasking offers significant advantages, it also requires careful planning and consideration. Choosing the right tasks for your LLM and designing an effective training strategy are crucial for success.

Ready to unleash the language ninja within your LLM? In the next section, we'll explore another powerful technique: transfer learning. Think of it as leveraging the wisdom of experienced athletes to accelerate your LLM's training journey!

5.2 Curriculum Learning & Data Augmentation: The Training Transformation

Imagine crafting the perfect training regimen for your athlete, starting with basic drills and gradually progressing to complex maneuvers. This is the essence of curriculum learning, a technique that transforms your LLM's training journey, unlocking its full potential. Let's explore how curriculum learning, combined with the power of data augmentation, empowers your LLM to achieve mastery!

Shaping the Learning Curve: Curriculum Learning

Think of curriculum learning as guiding your athlete through an educational journey. You wouldn't throw them into the deep end immediately, right? Instead, you'd start with foundational skills and gradually introduce more challenging concepts.

Similarly, curriculum learning involves presenting the LLM with training data in increasing order of difficulty. This starts with simpler examples and gradually progresses to more complex ones. By carefully sequencing the learning material, you help the LLM:

- Avoid getting stuck in local optima: Imagine your athlete getting fixated on one training technique that hinders their progress. Curriculum learning prevents this by introducing new challenges that nudge them towards better solutions.

- Grasp complex concepts more effectively: By building a strong foundation, the LLM can more easily understand and apply the knowledge from more challenging examples later in the training process.
- Achieve better overall performance: By ensuring a smooth and efficient learning curve, curriculum learning helps your LLM reach its full potential.

Data Augmentation: Expanding the Training Grounds

Imagine having a limited training space for your athlete, hindering their overall development. Data augmentation tackles this challenge by artificially expanding your training data, creating a richer and more diverse learning environment for your LLM.

Think of it like providing your athlete with a variety of training drills that mimic real-world scenarios. Here are some common data augmentation techniques:

- Synonym replacement: Replacing words with synonyms to expose the LLM to different phrasings of the same concept.
- Back-translation: Machine translating the training data into another language and then back to the original language, introducing variations in sentence structure and vocabulary.
- Sentence shuffling: Randomly shuffling the order of words within a sentence, encouraging the LLM to focus on word meaning and context.

By incorporating data augmentation, you:

- Reduce overfitting: The LLM learns from a wider range of examples, making it less prone to memorizing specific patterns in the training data.

- Improvegeneralizability: The LLM becomes more adaptable to unseen data and real-world situations.
- Enhance robustness: The exposure to diverse data variations makes the LLM more resilient to noise and errors in the input data.

Remember: Both curriculum learning and data augmentation are powerful tools, but they require careful implementation tailored to

your specific task and LLM architecture. Experiment and analyze the results to find the optimal approach for your needs.

Ready to witness your LLM's training transformed? In the next section, we'll delve into the fascinating world of custom loss functions and metrics, empowering you to fine-tune your LLM's learning process with even greater precision!

Imagine taking your athlete from basic drills to championship-level performance. That's the power of curriculum learning and data augmentation, techniques that transform your LLM's training journey, unlocking its full potential. Let's explore how these methods, combined with code examples, empower your LLM to achieve mastery!

Shaping the Learning Curve: Curriculum Learning

Concept: Gradually increase the difficulty of training data presented to your LLM.

Benefits:

- Avoid local optima (getting stuck on ineffective solutions)

- Grasp complex concepts more effectively
- Achieve better overall performance

Example (Text summarization):

1. Start with short, simple news articles with clear summaries.
2. Gradually progress to longer, more complex articles with multi-faceted summaries.
3. Introduce articles with missing information or ambiguous language, requiring deeper understanding.

Code example (PyTorch):

Python

```python
# Define difficulty levels based on sentence
length or complexity metrics

difficulty_levels = [1, 2, 3]



# Start with the easiest level

current_level = 0



for epoch in range(num_epochs):

    # Train on examples from the current difficulty
level
```

```
for data in
train_data_loader[difficulty_levels[current_level
]]:

    # ... training loop ...



  # Increase difficulty level after specified
epochs

  if epoch % increase_difficulty_every == 0:

    current_level += 1
```

Data Augmentation: Expanding the Training Grounds

Concept: Artificially create new training data variations to improve diversity andgeneralizability.

Benefits:

- Reduce overfitting
- Improvegeneralizability
- Enhance robustness to noise and errors

Examples:

- Synonym replacement: Replace words with synonyms (e.g., "happy" -> "joyful").
- Back-translation: Translate data to another language and back, introducing variations.
- Sentence shuffling: Randomly shuffle word order within sentences.
- Textual perturbations: Add typos, noise, or grammatical errors.

Code example (Transformers library):

Python

```python
from transformers import AutoTokenizer




tokenizer =
AutoTokenizer.from_pretrained("bert-base-uncased"
)




def augment_text(text):

  # Apply synonym replacement

  augmented_text = tokenizer.augment_tokens(text,
num_beams=2)

  # Back-translate (requires additional
libraries)
```

```python
  # ...

  # Textual perturbations

  # ...

  return augmented_text


# Apply augmentation during training

for data in train_data:

  text, label = data

  augmented_text = augment_text(text)

  # Train on augmented text and label

  # ...
```

Remember: Adapt these examples to your specific task and LLM architecture. Experiment with different techniques and hyperparameters to find the optimal approach for your needs.

Ready to witness your LLM's training transformed? In the next section, we'll delve into the fascinating world of custom loss functions and metrics, empowering you to fine-tune your LLM's learning process with even greater precision!

5.3 Customizing the Scoreboard: Beyond the Standard Metrics

Imagine evaluating a gymnast's routine solely on the number of flips. Standard metrics like accuracy and precision are valuable tools in LLM evaluation, but they often tell an incomplete story. Just like a well-crafted gymnastics scorecard considers artistry and execution, custom loss functions and metrics allow you to tailor evaluation to your specific LLM tasks, empowering you to become a true performance judge!

Why Customize?

Standard metrics offer a quick-and-dirty assessment, but they often miss crucial nuances. Consider sentiment analysis: accuracy might not capture your ability to identify sarcasm or subtle emotions. Customization empowers you to:

- Focus on what matters: Define your goals and desired outcomes. Is it factual accuracy, fluency, creativity, or something else entirely? Craft metrics that align with your priorities.
- Go beyond the obvious: Standard metrics often miss key aspects. For example, in dialogue generation, fluency and staying on topic might be more important than raw accuracy.
- Embrace creativity: Don't be afraid to get creative! Invent task-specific metrics that truly reflect your LLM's performance.

Examples and Applications:

- Sentiment analysis with emotional depth:
    - Standard accuracy measures overall correctness, but what about sarcasm detection?
    - Define a `sarcasm_accuracy` metric that specifically evaluates how well your LLM identifies sarcastic sentiment.

-

- Machine translation with a human touch:
    - BLEU score assesses translation quality, but fluency is also crucial.
    - Design a `fluency_score` metric that considers factors like sentence length, vocabulary complexity, and readability.

-

Remember: Crafting custom metrics requires effort and experimentation. Start by clearly understanding your task and LLM's goals. As you learn more about its strengths and weaknesses, refine your metrics for a more comprehensive evaluation.

Ready to become a master LLM performance judge? The next chapter dives into the exciting world of real-world LLM applications, showcasing how others have utilized these techniques to create groundbreaking solutions. Get inspired and see how your custom scoreboard can unlock the true potential of your LLMs!

While standard metrics like accuracy and precision are valuable tools, they often paint an incomplete picture of your LLM's performance. They're like judging a diving competition solely on the splash - it misses the grace, control, and difficulty of the execution. That's where custom loss functions and metrics come in. They empower you to design a personalized scoreboard that truly reflects the nuances of your task and your LLM's capabilities. Let's delve into this concept with examples and code, transforming you from a passive observer to an active performance evaluator!

Crafting a Meaningful Scoreboard:

- Know Your Goals: What truly matters in your LLM's performance? Is it factual accuracy, fluency, creativity, or something else entirely? Clearly define your objectives before crafting your custom metrics. Don't get stuck in the trap of blindly chasing generic metrics that don't align with your specific needs.
- Think Beyond the Obvious: Standard metrics often miss crucial aspects. For instance, in sentiment analysis, accuracy might not tell the whole story. You might care more about correctly identifying nuanced emotions like sarcasm or frustration. Don't be afraid to dig deeper and identify the hidden gems that truly reflect your LLM's strengths and weaknesses.
- Embrace Creativity: The world of custom metrics is your oyster! Consider task-specific metrics that go beyond the generic. In dialogue generation, you might measure the naturalness of conversation flow, the ability to stay on topic, or even the generation of humorous responses. Remember, the possibilities are endless!

Examples and Code:

- Sentiment Analysis with Emotional Nuance:

Imagine you're training an LLM to analyze customer reviews. While standard accuracy is important, you might also care about identifying:

*   **Sarcasm:**

Python

```python
# Standard accuracy metric
def standard_accuracy(predictions, labels):
  # ... (implementation of standard accuracy)

# Custom metric for sarcasm detection
def sarcasm_accuracy(predictions, labels):
  # Identify sarcastic examples in labels
  sarcastic_labels = [label for label, text in zip(labels, texts) if "!" in text]
  # Calculate accuracy only for sarcastic examples
  return standard_accuracy(predictions[sarcastic_labels], sarcastic_labels)

# Use both metrics during evaluation
standard_acc = standard_accuracy(predictions, labels)
sarcasm_acc = sarcasm_accuracy(predictions, labels)
print(f"Standard accuracy: {standard_acc}, Sarcasm accuracy: {sarcasm_acc}")
```

* **Frustration:**

Python

```python
# Custom metric for frustration detection using sentiment lexicons
def frustration_score(predictions, labels):
  frustration_lexicon = ["upset", "angry", "disappointed"]
  frustration_count = 0
  for i, (prediction, label) in enumerate(zip(predictions, labels)):
    if prediction == "negative" and any(word in texts[i] for word in frustration_lexicon):
      frustration_count += 1
  return frustration_count / len(labels)

# Combine metrics for comprehensive evaluation
standard_acc = standard_accuracy(predictions, labels)
sarcasm_acc = sarcasm_accuracy(predictions, labels)
frustration_score = frustration_score(predictions, labels)
print(f"Standard accuracy: {standard_acc}, Sarcasm accuracy: {sarcasm_acc}, Frustration score: {frustration_score}")
```

- Machine Translation with Human-like Fluency:

BLEU score is a common metric for translation quality, but it doesn't capture human-like fluency. Consider incorporating:

* **Sentence length variation:**

Python

```
# Custom metric for sentence length variation
def sentence_length_variation(translations):
    sentence_lengths = [len(sent.split()) for sent
in translations]
    return np.std(sentence_lengths)

# Combine metrics for a more holistic evaluation
bleu_score = bleu_score(generated_translations,
original_texts)
fluency_score =
sentence_length_variation(generated_translations)
print(f"BLEU score: {bleu_score}, Fluency score:
{fluency_score}")
```

Remember: Crafting custom metrics is an iterative process. Start with a clear understanding of your task and gradually evolve your metrics as you learn more about your LLM's performance. Don't be afraid to experiment and get creative!

Ready to become a master evaluator of your LLM's performance? The next chapter dives into the exciting world of real-world LLM applications, showcasing how others have used these techniques to create groundbreaking solutions. Get inspired and see how your custom scoreboard can empower you

Chapter 6: Unleashing Your Inner LLM Architect: Building with Transformers!

Ready to ditch the training wheels and dive into the thrilling world of custom LLM architecture? Buckle up, language enthusiasts, because this chapter empowers you to become a full-fledged LLM architect, wielding the mighty Transformer like a pro!

6.1 Transformer Tales: A Tour of the Titans

Before we dive into the thrilling world of building your own LLM architecture, let's take a tour of the key players: Transformer variants. Think of them as the essential building blocks, each with unique strengths and specializations. Understanding their characteristics will empower you to make informed decisions when constructing your LLM masterpiece!

The Transformer Legacy:

- The Original Transformer: The foundation of it all, the vanilla Transformer architecture rose to fame for its prowess in machine translation and text summarization. Its encoder-decoder structure efficiently handles sequence-to-sequence tasks, making it a versatile starting point.

Pre-trained Powerhouses:

- BERT & RoBERTa: These pre-trained giants excel at understanding the nuances and relationships within language. Imagine them as experts in contextual awareness, making them perfect for tasks like question answering and natural language inference. Their ability to grasp deeper meaning empowers them to excel in tasks that require comprehension beyond just surface-level understanding.
- BART: If multilingualism is your goal, BART is your champion. This versatile Transformer tackles not only translation across languages but also shines in generating creative text formats, like poems and even code! Its fluency in diverse languages and creative domains makes it a valuable asset for projects requiring both linguistic dexterity and artistic flair.

The Multitasking Marvel:

- T5: The ultimate multitasker, T5 boasts impressive adaptability across various domains. Think of it as a master chef who can whip up a delicious dish regardless of the ingredients. This flexibility makes it suitable for diverse tasks, from text summarization to question answering, demonstrating its general-purpose problem-solving prowess.

Remember: This is just a glimpse into the Transformer family. As you explore further, you'll discover even more specialized variants, each fine-tuned for specific tasks and domains. Choosing the right tool for the job is crucial for success!

In the next section, we'll move from understanding these Transformers to actually using them to design and build your own custom LLM architecture. Get ready to unleash your inner architect and bring your language processing dreams to life!

Before we embark on the exciting journey of constructing your own LLM architecture, let's meet the essential building blocks: Transformer variants. Each brings unique strengths and skills to the table, and understanding them will empower you to choose the right tools for your LLM masterpiece!

The Transformer Legacy:

- The Original Transformer: The foundational hero, the vanilla Transformer (Vaswani et al., 2017) conquered the machine translation world with its encoder-decoder architecture. Imagine an encoder that reads and understands an input sentence (think of it as learning the gist) and a decoder that translates that understanding into another language. This core structure makes it versatile for various sequence-to-sequence tasks.

Pre-trained Powerhouses:

- BERT & RoBERTa: These pre-trained titans, BERT (Devlin et al., 2018) and RoBERTa (Liu et al., 2019), are masters of contextual awareness. Think of them as language experts who have devoured massive amounts of text and can now understand the subtle nuances and relationships between words. This expertise shines in tasks like question answering:

Python

```
from transformers import BertTokenizer,
BertForQuestionAnswering
```

```python
# Load pre-trained model and tokenizer
tokenizer =
BertTokenizer.from_pretrained('bert-base-uncased'
)
model =
BertForQuestionAnswering.from_pretrained('bert-ba
se-uncased')

# Prepare question and context
question = "What is the capital of France?"
context = "France is a country located in Western
Europe. Its capital is Paris, a major European
city and global center for art, fashion, and
gastronomy."

# Tokenize and encode
encoded_inputs = tokenizer(question, context,
return_tensors='pt')

# Ask the model and interpret the answer
outputs = model(**encoded_inputs)
start_scores, end_scores = outputs[0], outputs[1]

answer_start = torch.argmax(start_scores)
answer_end = torch.argmax(end_scores) + 1

answer = context[answer_start:answer_end]
print(f"Question: {question}\nAnswer: {answer}")
```

- BART: If multilingualism is your quest, BART (Lewis et al., 2019) is your champion. Not only can it translate between languages, but it can also generate different creative text formats like poems and code! Its fluency in diverse domains makes it a valuable asset:

Python

```python
from transformers import BartTokenizer,
BartForConditionalGeneration

# Load pre-trained model and tokenizer
tokenizer =
BartTokenizer.from_pretrained('facebook/bart-base
')
model =
BartForConditionalGeneration.from_pretrained('fac
ebook/bart-base')

# Generate poem about nature
prompt = "Write a poem about the beauty of a
sunrise."

# Generate text
generated_poem =
model.generate(input_ids=tokenizer.encode(prompt,
return_tensors='pt'))

# Decode and print the poem
print(tokenizer.decode(generated_poem[0],
skip_special_tokens=True))
```

The Multitasking Marvel:

- T5: The ultimate multitasker, T5 (Raffel et al., 2020), adapts to various domains like a culinary master adapting recipes. Imagine it trained on a massive dataset of different tasks, enabling it to approach new challenges with impressive flexibility. Here's an example of text summarization:

Python

```python
from transformers import T5Tokenizer,
T5ForConditionalGeneration

# Load pre-trained model and tokenizer
tokenizer =
T5Tokenizer.from_pretrained('t5-base')
model =
T5ForConditionalGeneration.from_pretrained('t5-ba
se')

# Prepare article and desired summary length
article = "This is a long and informative article
about the history of artificial intelligence."
summary_length = 50

# Generate summary
encoded_text = tokenizer(article,
return_tensors='pt')
```

```python
summary_ids =
model.generate(input_ids=encoded_text['input_ids'
], num_beams=4, max_length=summary_length)

# Decode and print the summary
summary = tokenizer.decode(summary_ids[0],
skip_special_tokens=True)
print(f"Original
Article:\n{article}\nSummary:\n{summary}")
```

Remember: This is just a taste of the Transformer family. As you explore further, you'll discover even more specialized variants, each with its own unique skillset. Choosing the right one for your specific task is key to building a successful LLM!

6.2 Architecting Your Dream LLM: From Blueprint to Reality

Now that you've met the Transformer titans, it's time to unleash your inner architect and design your very own LLM masterpiece! Think of it as sketching your dream house – what features will it have, how will it function, and what problems will it solve? Buckle up, because we're about to transform from curious observers into creative builders.

1. Define Your Mission:

Before laying the first digital brick, ask yourself: what problem are you trying to solve with your LLM? Is it generating realistic dialogue for chatbots, translating languages with nuanced understanding, or writing creative content that rivals human authors? Clearly defining your mission is crucial for choosing the right tools and techniques.

2. Select Your Transformer Heroes:

Remember the Transformer variants you met in the previous section? Each has its strengths and weaknesses. Based on your mission, choose the Transformer(s) that best align with your needs. Consider factors like:

- Pre-training: Have they been trained on massive datasets, giving them general language understanding? (e.g., BERT, RoBERTa)
- Task-specific capabilities: Are they fine-tuned for a specific task similar to yours? (e.g., T5 for summarization, BART for translation)
- Computational efficiency: How much processing power and memory do you have available? (e.g., smaller Transformers like T5-small vs. larger models like BART-base)

3. Stack & Customize: Unleash Your Creativity:

Don't just copy and paste pre-existing models! The beauty of custom architecture lies in its flexibility. Here's where you can truly shine:

- Stack Transformer layers: Experiment with adding or removing layers to adjust the model's complexity and capacity for learning. More layers often improve performance, but also require more computational resources.

- Customize encoder/decoder structure: If your task involves specific input and output formats, tailor the encoder and decoder accordingly. For example, a text summarization model might have a different decoder structure than a machine translation model.
- Fine-tune hyperparameters: These are the dials and levers that control the learning process. Experiment with learning rate, batch size, and other parameters to optimize your model's performance for your specific task.

Remember, there's no one-size-fits-all solution. Embrace the iterative process: build, test, analyze, and refine! The journey of creating your perfect LLM is half the fun!

Ready to see your dream LLM come to life? In the next section, we'll delve into the exciting world of training and evaluation. We'll equip you with the tools to turn your architectural masterpiece into a language processing powerhouse!

6.3 Training & Evaluating: From Apprentice to Master

You've meticulously designed your LLM architecture, a testament to your creativity and problem-solving skills. Now it's time to bring it to life through the transformative power of training and evaluation. Think of it as nurturing your fledgling LLM from an eager apprentice to a language processing master!

1. Gather Your Data: The Fuel for Learning

Just like any apprentice, your LLM needs the right fuel to learn and grow: high-quality data. Remember, the quality and quantity of your data significantly impact your LLM's performance. Here are some key considerations:

- Relevance: Ensure your data aligns with your task and target audience. For example, training a customer service chatbot on medical terminology would likely not be optimal.
- Diversity: Expose your LLM to diverse examples to prevent overfitting and enhance its ability to generalize to unseen data.
- Volume: Generally, more data leads to better performance, but it's also about finding the right balance for your resources and computational capacity.

2. Craft Your Training Regimen: Shaping the Learner

Training isn't just about throwing data at your LLM. You need a well-designed training regimen to optimize learning:

- Loss function: This function measures the difference between the LLM's predictions and the desired outcomes.

Choose a loss function that accurately reflects your task goals (e.g., cross-entropy loss for classification tasks).

- Optimizer: This algorithm adjusts the LLM's internal parameters to minimize the loss function. Popular optimizers include Adam and SGD, each with its advantages and disadvantages.
- Learning rate: This controls how much the LLM's parameters change in each training step. Start with a higher learning rate for faster initial learning and gradually decrease it for fine-tuning.

3. Evaluate & Refine: The Path to Mastery

Don't just hope for the best! Continuously evaluate your LLM's performance using relevant metrics and qualitative analysis:

- Quantitative metrics: Use metrics like accuracy, precision, recall, and F1-score to assess your LLM's performance on a held-out validation set.
- Qualitative analysis: Manually evaluate the LLM's outputs for fluency, coherence, and alignment with your task goals.

Based on your evaluation results, refine your architecture, training process, and data selection. This iterative process is crucial for guiding your LLM towards mastery.

Remember: Training LLMs is an ongoing journey of exploration and discovery. Be patient, persistent, and celebrate your milestones. As you iterate and improve, you'll witness your LLM blossom into a powerful language processing master, ready to tackle real-world challenges!

Ready to unleash your LLM's potential on the world? In the next chapter, we'll explore the captivating world of real-world LLM applications. See how others have used these techniques to create groundbreaking solutions that are changing the world! Get ready to be inspired and discover the endless possibilities that await you in the realm of custom LLM architecture.

You've meticulously designed your LLM architecture, a testament to your creativity and problem-solving prowess. Now, it's time to breathe life into your creation through the transformative power of training and evaluation. Think of it as guiding your LLM from an eager apprentice to a language processing master!

1. Gather Your Data: Fueling the Learning Journey

Just like any apprentice, your LLM needs the right data to learn and grow. Remember, the quality and quantity significantly impact its performance. Here are some key considerations:

- Relevance: Ensure your data aligns with your task and target audience. Training a customer service chatbot on medical terminology wouldn't be ideal. For example, if you're building a sentiment analysis LLM, gather tweets or reviews expressing different emotions.
- Diversity: Expose your LLM to diverse examples to prevent overfitting and enhance its ability to generalize to unseen data. Don't just feed it positive reviews if you want it to identify negative sentiment accurately.
- Volume: Generally, more data leads to better performance, but there's a balance to consider. Start with a manageable amount and scale up gradually based on your resources and computational capacity.

Example: Let's say you're building a chatbot for a music streaming service. You might gather:

- User reviews of different music genres and artists.
- Transcripts of customer service conversations related to music recommendations.
- Social media posts discussing music preferences.

2. Craft Your Training Regimen: Shaping the Learner

Training isn't just about throwing data at your LLM. You need a well-designed training regimen to optimize learning:

- Loss function: This measures the difference between the LLM's predictions and the desired outcomes. Choose one that reflects your task goals. For sentiment analysis, you might use binary cross-entropy loss to distinguish positive and negative sentiment.
- Optimizer: This algorithm adjusts the LLM's internal parameters to minimize the loss function. Popular choices include Adam and SGD. Adam often converges faster, while SGD can be more fine-tuned.
- Learning rate: This controls how much the parameters change in each training step. Start with a higher rate for faster initial learning and gradually decrease it for fine-tuning.

Example Code (using PyTorch for sentiment analysis):

Python

```python
from transformers import BertTokenizer,
BertForSequenceClassification

# Load pre-trained model and tokenizer
```

```python
tokenizer =
BertTokenizer.from_pretrained('bert-base-uncased'
)
model =
BertForSequenceClassification.from_pretrained('be
rt-base-uncased', num_labels=2)  # 2 for binary
sentiment

# Define loss function and optimizer
loss_fn = nn.CrossEntropyLoss()
optimizer = torch.optim.AdamW(model.parameters(),
lr=2e-5)

# Training loop
for epoch in range(3):
  # ... (load and process training data)
  for batch in data:
    # Forward pass
    outputs = model(**batch)
    loss = loss_fn(outputs.logits, labels)

    # Backward pass and optimization
    loss.backward()
    optimizer.step()
    optimizer.zero_grad()

# Evaluate on held-out validation set
# ... (implement evaluation metrics like
accuracy)
```

3. Evaluate & Refine: The Path to Mastery

Don't just hope for the best! Continuously evaluate your LLM's performance using relevant metrics and qualitative analysis:

- Quantitative metrics: Use metrics like accuracy, precision, recall, and F1-score to assess performance on a held-out validation set. Track these metrics across training epochs to monitor progress.
- Qualitative analysis: Manually evaluate the LLM's outputs for fluency, coherence, and alignment with your task goals. Does it generate human-like responses in the case of a chatbot, or provide accurate sentiment classifications?

Based on your evaluation results, refine your architecture, training process, and data selection. This iterative process is crucial for guiding your LLM towards mastery.

Remember: Training LLMs is an ongoing journey of exploration and discovery. Be patient, persistent, and celebrate your milestones. As you iterate and improve, you'll witness your LLM blossom into a powerful language processing master, ready to tackle real-world challenges!

Ready to unleash your LLM's potential on the world? In the next chapter, we'll explore the captivating world of real-world LLM applications. See how others have used these techniques to create groundbreaking solutions that are changing the world! Get ready to be inspired and discover the endless possibilities that await you in the realm of custom LLM architecture.

Chapter 7: Unleashing Your LLM: From Lab to Launchpad!

Congratulations, language maestro! You've crafted your very own LLM masterpiece, honed its skills through rigorous training, and now it's time to unleash its power on the world! But before you set it loose like a digital genie, let's explore the thrilling realm of integrating your LLM into real-world applications. Buckle up, because we're about to transform your LLM from a solo performer to a collaborative star!

7.1 Choosing Your Stage: Finding the Perfect Deployment Platform

Imagine your custom-built LLM, a marvel of language processing prowess, ready to shine on the world stage. But where will it perform? Choosing the right deployment platform is crucial for maximizing your LLM's impact and ensuring a seamless audience experience. Let's explore the different options, each offering unique advantages:

1. Cloud Providers: Scalability & Accessibility

Think of cloud giants like AWS, Azure, and Google Cloud as massive concert halls, catering to vast audiences. They offer:

- Scalability: Easily adjust resources based on your LLM's traffic and processing demands, ensuring smooth performance even during peak usage.
- Accessibility: Deploy your LLM globally with minimal infrastructure setup, making it readily available to users worldwide.

- Managed services: Leverage pre-built tools and services for tasks like load balancing and security, simplifying deployment and management.

Consider cloud platforms if:

- You anticipate high user traffic or fluctuating demand.
- You need global reach and easy accessibility for your LLM.
- You prefer a managed service approach with minimal infrastructure setup.

2. Edge Computing: Low Latency & Offline Capabilities

Imagine your LLM performing directly at the audience's fingertips, like a local band rocking a cozy club. Edge computing brings the show closer with:

- Low latency: Process data and generate responses near the user, minimizing delays and ensuring real-time interaction.
- Offline capabilities: Enable your LLM to function even without internet connectivity, crucial for applications like chatbots on smart devices.
- Reduced costs: Process data locally, potentially minimizing reliance on expensive cloud resources.

Consider edge computing if:

- Your LLM application requires low latency and real-time responses.
- Offline functionality is essential, like for chatbots on mobile devices.
- Cost optimization is a major concern.

3. Specialized Platforms: Tailored Solutions

Think of these platforms as dedicated music studios, catering to specific LLM needs. Options like Hugging Face Hub and NVIDIA Triton Inference Server offer:

- Fine-tuned tools: Specialized features and optimizations designed for LLMs, potentially improving performance and efficiency.
- Community support: Access to communities of LLM developers and experts for collaboration and troubleshooting.
- Flexibility: Tailor the deployment environment to your specific LLM architecture and requirements.

Consider specialized platforms if:

- Your LLM has unique needs not fully met by generic platforms.
- You value access to a specialized LLM community and expertise.
- You require fine-grained control over the deployment environment.

Remember, the perfect platform depends on your LLM's specific requirements and the audience you want to reach. Carefully evaluate factors like scalability, latency, cost, and community support to choose the stage that will amplify your LLM's impact and ensure a flawless performance!

Imagine your custom-built LLM, a marvel of language processing, ready to shine on the world stage. But where will it perform? Choosing the right deployment platform is crucial for maximizing its impact and ensuring a seamless audience experience. Let's explore options, each offering unique advantages, with examples and code snippets to illustrate:

1. Cloud Providers: Scalability & Accessibility

Think of cloud giants like AWS, Azure, and Google Cloud as massive concert halls, catering to vast audiences. They offer:

- Scalability:
    - Example: Imagine your LLM powers a chatbot for a large e-commerce platform. On Black Friday, traffic spikes massively. With AWS Auto Scaling, your LLM seamlessly scales up resources to handle the surge, ensuring smooth performance for all users.
    -
    - Code snippet (AWS, simplified):
    -
- Python

```
from aws_cdk import core as cdk

from aws_cdk import aws_autoscaling as autoscaling



# Define instance type and desired capacity range
```

```python
instance_type = ec2.InstanceType.of(

    ec2.InstanceClass.T3, ec2.InstanceSize.LARGE

)

min_capacity = 2

max_capacity = 10



# Create Auto Scaling group for your LLM
instances

my_asg = autoscaling.AutoScalingGroup(

    scope=self,

    id="MyLLMASG",

    instance_type=instance_type,

    min_capacity=min_capacity,

    max_capacity=max_capacity,

)
```

-
-

- Accessibility:
  - Example: You deploy your LLM as a sentiment analysis API globally. With Azure Content Delivery Network (CDN), users worldwide can access the API with low latency, regardless of their location.

-
- Managed services:
  - Example: You leverage Google Cloud AI Platform for simplified deployment and management. It handles tasks like load balancing and security, freeing you to focus on your LLM's core functionality.

-

Consider cloud platforms if:

- You anticipate high user traffic or fluctuating demand.
- You need global reach and easy accessibility for your LLM.
- You prefer a managed service approach with minimal infrastructure setup.

2. Edge Computing: Low Latency & Offline Capabilities

Imagine your LLM performing directly at the audience's fingertips, like a local band rocking a cozy club. Edge computing brings the show closer with:

- Low latency:
  - Example: Your LLM powers a real-time voice assistant on a smart speaker. Edge computing minimizes processing delays, ensuring instant responses to user queries.

-
- Offline capabilities:

- Example: You deploy your LLM on a mobile device for offline language translation. Edge computing enables the LLM to function even without internet connectivity.
-
- Reduced costs:
  - Example: You process data locally on smart devices instead of relying on cloud resources, potentially reducing costs.
-

Consider edge computing if:

- Your LLM application requires low latency and real-time responses.
- Offline functionality is essential, like for chatbots on mobile devices.
- Cost optimization is a major concern.

3. Specialized Platforms: Tailored Solutions

Think of these platforms as dedicated music studios, catering to specific LLM needs. Options like Hugging Face Hub and NVIDIA Triton Inference Server offer:

- Fine-tuned tools:
  - Example: You use Hugging Face Hub for fine-tuning your LLM on a specific task like medical code generation. Their platform provides tools and datasets optimized for healthcare LLMs.
-
- Community support:

- ○ Example: You leverage the NVIDIA Triton Inference Server community forum to troubleshoot deployment issues and learn from other LLM developers.
-
- Flexibility:
  - ○ Example: You customize the deployment environment on NVIDIA Triton Inference Server to optimize performance for your unique LLM architecture.
-

Consider specialized platforms if:

- Your LLM has unique needs not fully met by generic platforms.
- You value access to a specialized LLM community and expertise.
- You require fine-grained control over the deployment environment.

Remember, the perfect platform depends on your LLM's specific requirements and the audience you want to reach. Carefully evaluate factors like scalability, latency, cost, and community support to choose the stage that will amplify your LLM's impact and ensure a flawless performance!

7.2 APIs & Workflows: The Seamless Symphony

So, your LLM's on the perfect platform, ready to dazzle the audience. But how will it interact with the outside world? That's where APIs (Application Programming Interfaces) come in, acting as the sheet music that tells your LLM what to do. Imagine a conductor guiding an orchestra – with clear instructions from the API, your LLM can seamlessly integrate into various applications.

But don't forget the unsung heroes: workflows. These automated processes handle the behind-the-scenes magic, ensuring everything runs smoothly. Think of them as the stage crew, preparing data, feeding it to the LLM, and delivering the results flawlessly.

Understanding APIs:

- API acts as a messenger: It receives requests containing data (like text or audio) from other applications.
- Clear instructions: The API translates the request into a format your LLM understands.
- LLM does its magic: Your LLM processes the data based on the API's instructions, generating text, translation, or other outputs.
- API delivers the results: The API translates the LLM's output back into a format understandable by the requesting application.

Workflows: The Unsung Heroes:

- Data preparation: Before the LLM takes center stage, workflows ensure the data is clean, pre-processed, and formatted correctly.
- Model inference: They feed the prepared data to the LLM, ensuring smooth interaction.
- Output delivery: Once the LLM works its magic, workflows handle the final results, sending them back to the requesting application.

Together, APIs and workflows create a seamless symphony, enabling your LLM to collaborate effortlessly with other applications.

Remember:

- Choose the right API design: Consider factors like authentication, security, and versioning to ensure robust communication.
- Design efficient workflows: Optimize data handling and minimize latency for a smooth user experience.

With well-designed APIs and efficient workflows, your LLM will be ready to rock any application, captivating audiences with its linguistic prowess!

Imagine your LLM, a virtuoso of language, gracing the stage. But how does it interact with the outside world? Here's where the magic of APIs (Application Programming Interfaces) and workflows comes in, ensuring a seamless performance.

APIs: The Conductor's Baton

Think of APIs as the clear instructions a conductor gives the orchestra. They act as intermediaries:

- Receiving requests: They accept data (text, audio, etc.) from other applications in a structured format.
- Translating requests: The API converts the request into a format your LLM understands, specifying the task and desired output.

- Delivering results: After the LLM works its magic, the API translates its output back into a human-readable format and sends it back to the requesting application.

Example (Sentiment analysis API using Flask):

Python

```python
from flask import Flask, request, jsonify



app = Flask(__name__)



@app.route('/api/sentiment', methods=['POST'])

def analyze_sentiment():

  text = request.json['text']

  # Pass text to your LLM for sentiment analysis

  sentiment = your_llm.predict(text)

  # Return sentiment as JSON response

  return jsonify({'sentiment': sentiment})
```

```
if __name__ == '__main__':

    app.run(debug=True)
```

Workflows: The Stage Crew in Action

While the API conducts the interaction, workflows handle the behind-the-scenes magic:

- Data preparation: They ensure the incoming data is clean, pre-processed, and formatted correctly for your LLM.
- Model inference: They feed the prepared data to your LLM, ensuring smooth communication and efficient resource utilization.
- Output delivery: Once the LLM generates its response, workflows handle post-processing and send the final results back to the application.

Example (Workflow for image caption generation):

1. User uploads an image to a web application.
2. Workflow pre-processes the image (resize, format conversion).
3. Workflow sends the image data to your LLM for caption generation.
4. LLM generates a caption based on the image content.
5. Workflow post-processes the caption (grammar check, formatting).
6. Workflow displays the final caption alongside the image on the web app.

Remember:

- API design matters: Choose the right design principles for authentication, security, and versioning.
- Workflow efficiency is key: Optimize data handling and minimize latency for a smooth user experience.

With well-designed APIs and efficient workflows, your LLM becomes a maestro, collaborating seamlessly with various applications and captivating audiences with its linguistic prowess!

7.3 Case Studies: LLMs Take Center Stage - From Healthcare to Hollywood (with Examples & Code)

The applause roars as LLMs step into the spotlight, showcasing their versatility across diverse industries. Let's explore some real-world applications with concrete examples and code snippets:

Healthcare:

- Babylon Health: Their "Ask Babylon" symptom checker utilizes an LLM trained on vast medical literature. Users describe symptoms, and the LLM generates potential diagnoses and care recommendations (with disclaimers, emphasizing the need for professional consultation).

Example Code (Simplified):

Python

```python
# User enters symptoms (fever, cough, fatigue)
user_symptoms = ["fever", "cough", "fatigue"]
```

```
# Preprocess symptoms (text cleaning,
normalization)
preprocessed_symptoms =
preprocess_symptoms(user_symptoms)

# Pass preprocessed symptoms to LLM for diagnosis
suggestion
suggested_diagnoses =
llm_model.predict(preprocessed_symptoms)

# Filter and refine diagnoses based on medical
knowledge base
refined_diagnoses =
filter_diagnoses(suggested_diagnoses)

# Present results with clear disclaimers and
encourage consultation
present_results(refined_diagnoses, "Disclaimer:
Seek professional advice...")
```

- MedChat: This AI-powered chatbot uses an LLM to answer patients' medical questions in a conversational manner, providing reliable information and directing them to appropriate resources.

Finance:

- JPMorgan Chase: Their "COIN" system (Cognitive Open Information Network) leverages LLMs to analyze financial news, social media chatter, and other data sources to identify emerging trends and potential risks.

Example Code (Simplified):

Python

```
# Collect financial data (news articles, social
media sentiment)
financial_data = collect_data()

# Preprocess data (entity recognition, topic
modeling)
preprocessed_data =
preprocess_data(financial_data)

# Train LLM on preprocessed data to identify
financial patterns
train_llm_model(preprocessed_data)

# Use trained LLM to analyze new data and
identify potential risks
new_data = collect_new_data()
risks = llm_model.predict_risks(new_data)

# Generate report highlighting potential risks
and market trends
generate_report(risks)
```

Customer Service:

- Ada: This healthcare chatbot utilizes an LLM to understand user symptoms, answer questions, and guide them towards appropriate care options.

Entertainment:

- Netflix: They leverage LLMs to personalize content recommendations based on user viewing history, demographics, and other factors.

Remember, these are simplified examples. Real-world LLM applications involve complex models, data pipelines, and ethical considerations. As you explore the exciting potential of LLMs, keep these in mind:

- Focus on real-world impact: Align your LLM development with meaningful problems and positive contributions to society.
- Address ethical concerns: Ensure inclusivity, fairness, and transparency in your LLM design and applications.
- Embrace continuous learning: The LLM landscape is evolving rapidly, stay updated and keep learning to push the boundaries of what's possible.

So, take center stage! Leverage the power of LLMs to create innovative solutions, shape the future, and leave your unique mark on the world!

Chapter 8: Navigating the Ethical Maze: LLMs and the Responsibility We Share

So, you've crafted your LLM masterpiece, ready to conquer the world with its linguistic superpowers. But hold on, maestro! Before unleashing your creation, let's delve into the crucial realm of responsible AI and ethical considerations. Remember, with great power comes great responsibility, and LLMs are no exception.

8.1 Bias & Fairness: Unmasking the Hidden Skeletons in Your LLM

Imagine your LLM, a marvel of language processing, confidently generating text, translating languages, or writing code. But what if, beneath its impressive facade, lurk hidden biases? Unfortunately, this isn't science fiction. LLMs trained on real-world data can inherit and amplify societal biases, leading to unfair and harmful outcomes. Let's explore this crucial aspect of bias and fairness in LLMs:

Understanding Bias:

- Bias: Prejudice reflected in data or algorithms, leading to unfair treatment of certain groups.
- Example: An LLM trained on news articles might associate certain professions with specific genders, perpetuating harmful stereotypes in its outputs.

Impact of Bias:

- Unfair discrimination: Biased LLMs can unfairly disadvantage individuals or groups in areas like loan approvals, job applications, or even criminal justice.
- Erosion of trust: Lack of fairness erodes trust in AI systems, hindering their adoption and potential benefits.

Combating Bias:

- Data debiasing: Analyze training data for biases in language representation, cultural nuances, and ensure diverse perspectives are included.
- Fairness-aware training: Employ algorithms that explicitly consider fairness metrics during training, mitigating bias amplification.
- Continuous monitoring: Regularly assess your LLM's outputs for fairness issues and adapt your training data and algorithms accordingly.

Remember: Addressing bias is an ongoing process. Be proactive, use diverse datasets, and implement fairness-aware techniques throughout your LLM development journey.

Key Considerations:

- Data quality is paramount: Garbage in, garbage out. High-quality, diverse, and de-biased data is essential for fair LLMs.
- Challenge your assumptions: Don't blindly accept the status quo. Question potential biases in your data, algorithms, and evaluation metrics.
- Be transparent and accountable: Communicate your efforts to address bias and be open to feedback from diverse stakeholders.

By taking these steps, you can ensure your LLM not only shines with linguistic prowess but also champions fairness and responsible AI practices.

Stay tuned for the next section, where we delve into the interpretability of LLMs, another crucial aspect of building trustworthy and ethical AI systems.

Imagine your LLM, a whiz kid of language, churning out text, translating languages, or crafting code with impressive fluency. But what if, beneath this veneer of brilliance, lurk hidden biases? As with any powerful tool, LLMs trained on real-world data can inherit and amplify societal biases, leading to unfair and harmful outcomes. Let's shed light on this crucial aspect of bias and fairness in LLMs:

Understanding Bias:

- Bias: Prejudice reflected in data or algorithms, leading to unfair treatment of certain groups.
- Example: An LLM trained on news articles might associate "doctor" with male pronouns more often, perpetuating gender stereotypes in its generated text.

Impact of Bias:

- Unfair discrimination: Biased LLMs can disadvantage individuals or groups in areas like loan approvals, job applications, or even criminal justice. Imagine an LLM used in resume screening unintentionally favoring resumes using stereotypically "masculine" language over those using "feminine" language, impacting hiring decisions.

- Erosion of trust: Lack of fairness erodes trust in AI systems, hindering their adoption and potential benefits. Users need to believe AI systems are treating everyone justly.

Combating Bias:

- Data debiasing: Analyze training data for biases. Tools like Google AI's "Dataset Fairness Metric Tool" can help identify and mitigate biases in language representation, cultural nuances, and ensure diverse perspectives are included.
-
- Fairness-aware training: Employ algorithms that explicitly consider fairness metrics during training, mitigating bias amplification. For example, techniques like "counterfactual fairness" can help identify and address situations where the model's prediction would change if the individual belonged to a different group.
-
- Continuous monitoring: Regularly assess your LLM's outputs for fairness issues. Libraries like IBM's "AI Fairness 360" offer tools to measure and analyze potential biases in your LLM's outputs. Adapt your training data and algorithms accordingly based on your findings.
-

Remember: Addressing bias is an ongoing process. Be proactive, use diverse datasets, and implement fairness-aware techniques throughout your LLM development journey.

Key Considerations:

- Data quality is paramount: Garbage in, garbage out. High-quality, diverse, and de-biased data is essential for fair

LLMs. Consider collecting data from various sources and demographics to ensure representativeness.

- Challenge your assumptions: Don't blindly accept the status quo. Question potential biases in your data, algorithms, and evaluation metrics. Regularly audit your LLM's outputs for fairness issues and be open to feedback from diverse stakeholders.
- Be transparent and accountable: Communicate your efforts to address bias and be open to feedback from diverse stakeholders. This builds trust and encourages responsible AI development.

By taking these steps, you can ensure your LLM not only shines with linguistic prowess but also champions fairness and responsible AI practices.

Stay tuned for the next section, where we delve into the interpretability of LLMs, another crucial aspect of building trustworthy and ethical AI systems.

8.2 Explainability & Interpretability: Demystifying the Magic Box of Your LLM

Imagine your LLM, a mysterious language maestro, generating text, translating languages, or writing code with uncanny accuracy. But how does it perform these feats? What factors contribute to its outputs? Here's where explainability and interpretability (XAI) come into play, shedding light on the inner workings of your LLM and fostering trust:

Understanding XAI:

- Explainability: Understanding the reasoning behind an LLM's outputs. Why did it suggest that movie based on your viewing history?
- Interpretability: Making the LLM's decision-making process understandable to humans. Peeking under the hood to see how it arrived at its answer.

Why is XAI crucial?

- Transparency: Users trust AI systems more when they understand how they work. XAI fosters trust and reduces concerns about "black box" algorithms.
- Debugging and improvement: By understanding how your LLM makes decisions, you can identify and fix errors, leading to better performance.
- Accountability: If an LLM's output has unintended consequences, XAI helps identify the factors responsible, enabling accountability.

Approaches to XAI:

- Feature importance: Analyze which features in the input data had the most significant impact on the LLM's output.
- Counterfactual explanations: Explore how the output would have changed if certain input features were different, providing insights into the LLM's reasoning.
- Attention mechanisms: Visualize which parts of the input data the LLM focused on when generating its output, offering clues into its thought process.

Remember: Perfect XAI for complex LLMs is an ongoing area of research. However, striving for explainability and interpretability is essential for responsible AI development.

Key Considerations:

- Tailor XAI to your audience: Explainability needs vary depending on the audience (users, developers, regulators). Consider who needs to understand the LLM's reasoning and what level of detail is appropriate.
- Explain limitations alongside capabilities: Be transparent about what your LLM can and cannot do, avoiding inflated claims or overstating its explainability.
- Use XAI for continuous improvement: Leverage XAI insights to iteratively improve your LLM's performance, fairness, and overall trustworthiness.

By embracing XAI, you can transform your LLM from a mysterious oracle into a transparent partner, building trust and enabling responsible AI innovation.

Stay tuned for the next section, where we explore building responsible and trustworthy AI applications, taking your LLM development journey to the next level!

Imagine your LLM, a linguistic prodigy, churning out text, translating languages, or writing code with impressive results. But how does it achieve this magic? What factors contribute to its outputs? Here's where explainability and interpretability (XAI) come in, shedding light on your LLM's inner workings and fostering trust:

Understanding XAI:

- Explainability: Unraveling the reasoning behind an LLM's outputs. Why did it recommend that specific restaurant based on your search query?
- Interpretability: Making the LLM's decision-making process understandable. Like peeking under the hood of a car to see how it works.

Why is XAI crucial?

- Transparency: Users trust AI systems more when they understand their logic. XAI builds trust and reduces concerns about opaque algorithms.
- Debugging and improvement: By understanding how your LLM makes decisions, you can identify and fix errors, leading to better performance.
- Accountability: If an LLM's output has unintended consequences, XAI helps pinpoint the responsible factors, enabling accountability.

Approaches to XAI:

- Feature importance: Analyze which input features had the most significant impact on the output. For example, in a sentiment analysis LLM, understanding which words contributed most to the positive/negative sentiment helps interpret its reasoning.
- Counterfactual explanations: Explore how the output would change if certain input features were different. Imagine an LLM's loan approval decision. XAI might show how a slightly higher credit score would have changed the outcome, providing insights into its decision-making criteria.

Example (Counterfactual explanation with LIME for image classification):

```python
Python

# Import libraries

import lime

from lime import lime_image


# Load your image classifier LLM

image_classifier = load_your_llm()


# Define the image to be explained

image = load_image("cat.jpg")


# Explain the prediction for the image using LIME

explainer = lime_image.LimeImageExplainer()

explanation = explainer.explain_instance(image,
image_classifier, top_labels=3)
```

```
# Visualize the explanation

explanation.as_pyplot_figure()
```

- Attention mechanisms: Visualize which parts of the input
  data the LLM focused on when generating its output.
  Imagine a machine translation LLM. Attention mechanisms
  can highlight the source sentence words that most
  influenced the translated words, offering clues into its
  translation process.

Remember: Perfect XAI for complex LLMs remains an active
research area. However, striving for explainability and
interpretability is essential for responsible AI development.

Key Considerations:

- Tailor XAI to your audience: Explainability needs vary
  depending on who needs to understand the LLM (users,
  developers, regulators). Consider their level of technical
  expertise and what level of detail is appropriate.
- Explain limitations alongside capabilities: Be transparent
  about your LLM's capabilities and limitations. Avoid
  overstating its explainability or making inflated claims.
- Use XAI for continuous improvement: Leverage XAI insights
  to iteratively improve your LLM's performance, fairness, and
  overall trustworthiness.

By embracing XAI, you can transform your LLM from a mysterious
oracle into a transparent partner, building trust and enabling
responsible AI innovation.

Stay tuned for the next section, where we explore building responsible and trustworthy AI applications, taking your LLM development journey to the next level!

8.3 Building Responsible & Trustworthy AI Applications: Your LLM's Ethical Compass

Your LLM might be a marvel of language processing, but its journey doesn't end there. It's crucial to integrate your creation into a responsible and trustworthy AI application. Think of it as equipping your LLM with an ethical compass, guiding its impact on the world.

Key Principles:

- Human Values: Align your LLM's goals and outputs with ethical principles like fairness, privacy, non-maleficence (avoiding harm). Imagine an LLM used in hiring decisions. It should prioritize candidate skills and qualifications, not perpetuate biases based on factors like gender or ethnicity.
- Human Oversight: Don't leave your LLM unsupervised! Implement human oversight mechanisms to monitor its behavior and intervene if necessary. For example, in a medical diagnosis LLM, human doctors should always have the final say.
- Transparency & Communication: Be transparent about your LLM's capabilities and limitations. Communicate openly with users and stakeholders about how it works and its potential impact. Imagine using an LLM for news generation. Clearly disclose that the generated text is AI-created and not factual news reporting.

Practical Steps:

- Impact Assessment: Conduct regular assessments of your LLM's societal and ethical impact. Consider potential risks and biases, and adapt your application accordingly.
- Privacy & Security: Ensure your LLM adheres to privacy regulations and safeguards user data. Implement robust security measures to protect against unauthorized access or misuse.
- Accountability: Establish clear lines of accountability for your LLM's actions. Who is responsible for its outputs and any potential harm they cause?

Remember: Building responsible AI applications is an ongoing process, not a one-time effort. Continuously evaluate your LLM's impact, adapt your development practices, and embrace ethical considerations as core principles.

Examples:

- Explainable AI (XAI): Make your LLM's decision-making process understandable, fostering trust and enabling users to challenge potentially biased outputs.
- Data Governance: Implement responsible data collection, storage, and usage practices to mitigate bias and ensure data privacy.
- Human-in-the-Loop Systems: Combine your LLM with human expertise for tasks requiring judgment, ethics, and social understanding.

By following these guidelines, you can ensure your LLM not only showcases its linguistic prowess but also contributes to a positive and responsible future for all.

Ready to explore the exciting frontiers of responsible AI and LLM applications? Buckle up, because the next chapter delves into cutting-edge research, future possibilities, and the ever-evolving landscape of language models!

Your LLM might be a whiz kid with words, crafting text, translating languages, or writing code with impressive fluency. But remember, with great power comes great responsibility. It's not just about what your LLM can do, but how it integrates into a responsible and trustworthy AI application. Think of it as equipping your LLM with an ethical compass, guiding its impact on the world.

Key Principles:

- Human Values: Ensure your LLM's goals and outputs align with ethical principles like fairness, privacy, and non-maleficence (avoiding harm). Imagine an LLM used in loan approvals. It should base decisions on financial data, not perpetuate biases based on factors like race or gender.

-
- Human Oversight: Don't let your LLM run wild! Implement human oversight mechanisms to monitor its behavior and intervene if necessary. For example, in an LLM-powered medical diagnosis system, human doctors should have the final say.

-
- Transparency & Communication: Be upfront about your LLM's capabilities and limitations. Clearly communicate with users and stakeholders about how it works and its potential impact. Imagine using an LLM for news generation.

Disclose that the generated text is AI-created and not factual news reporting.

-

Practical Steps:

- Impact Assessment: Regularly assess your LLM's societal and ethical impact. Consider potential risks and biases, and adapt your application accordingly. Tools like Google's AI Impact Assessment Framework can help guide this process.

-
- Privacy & Security: Ensure your LLM adheres to privacy regulations and safeguards user data. Implement robust security measures like encryption and access controls. Libraries like TensorFlow Privacy offer tools for privacy-preserving machine learning.

-
- Accountability: Establish clear lines of accountability for your LLM's actions. Who is responsible for its outputs and any potential harm they cause?

-

Examples:

- Explainable AI (XAI): Make your LLM's decision-making process understandable. For example, in a sentiment analysis LLM, highlight which words contributed most to the sentiment classification, allowing users to understand and potentially challenge biased outputs.

-
- Data Governance: Implement responsible data collection, storage, and usage practices. Utilize diverse datasets to mitigate bias and ensure data privacy. Tools like IBM's AI

Fairness 360 can help identify and mitigate potential biases in your data.

-
- Human-in-the-Loop Systems: Combine your LLM with human expertise for tasks requiring judgment, ethics, and social understanding. For instance, in a content moderation system, an LLM might flag potentially harmful content, but a human reviewer makes the final decision.
-

Remember: Building responsible AI applications is an ongoing journey. Continuously evaluate your LLM's impact, adapt your development practices, and embrace ethical considerations as core principles.

Here's a code example using IBM's AI Fairness 360 to analyze potential bias in your LLM's training data:

Python

```python
from aif360.datasets import AdultDataset

from aif360.metrics import BinaryEqualOpportunityLoss



# Load the adult income dataset

data = AdultDataset()
```

```python
# Define privileged and unprivileged groups

privileged_groups =
[data.protected_attribute_names[0]]  # Assuming
first attribute is protected (e.g., gender)



# Calculate fairness metrics

loss =
BinaryEqualOpportunityLoss(privileged=privileged_
groups)

metric = loss.metric(data)



# Print the fairness metric (lower is better)

print(f"Binary Equal Opportunity Loss: {metric}")
```

By following these guidelines and leveraging available tools, you can ensure your LLM is not just a linguistic marvel, but a force for good in the world.

Join us in the next chapter as we explore the thrilling frontiers of responsible AI and LLM applications! We'll delve into cutting-edge research, future possibilities, and the ever-evolving landscape of language models.

Chapter 9: The Future of LLMs: Buckle Up, Word Nerds, It's Gonna Be Epic!

Hold onto your syntax highlighters, language enthusiasts, because we're about to blast off into the future of LLMs! Buckle up for a whirlwind tour of emerging trends, exciting advancements, and mind-blowing possibilities that will redefine the way we interact with language and technology.

9.1 Emerging Trends & Advancements in the LLM Landscape: A Glimpse into the Future

The world of LLMs is on a thrilling trajectory, constantly evolving and pushing the boundaries of what's possible. Let's delve into some key trends and advancements that will shape the future of language models:

1. Multilingual Mastery: Imagine seamlessly translating between hundreds of languages, shattering communication barriers and fostering global understanding. This isn't science fiction – LLMs are actively acquiring multilingual capabilities, able to process and generate text in diverse languages. This opens doors to:

- Real-time communication: Imagine having fluid conversations with anyone, regardless of their native language. LLMs could translate on-the-fly, bridging cultural divides and promoting collaboration.

- Multilingual content creation: From marketing materials to educational resources, LLMs can cater to global audiences, ensuring wider reach and impact.
- Breaking down information silos: Accessing information in different languages becomes effortless, fostering knowledge sharing and cross-cultural understanding.

2. Embracing Multimodality: Text is no longer king! LLMs are expanding their horizons, learning to process and generate information across different modalities, creating richer and more interactive experiences. Imagine an LLM that:

- Analyzes videos and generates captions: Imagine summarizing a lecture or describing a scene in natural language, making multimedia content more accessible.
- Writes code based on natural language descriptions: This could revolutionize programming, allowing users to express their ideas in plain English and have the LLM translate them into functional code.
- Creates interactive stories that respond to user input: Imagine having a conversation with a fictional character, the narrative unfolding based on your choices and prompts.

3. Contextual Comprehension: Forget keyword matching! LLMs are getting smarter, grasping the nuances of context and intent, making their responses more relevant and human-like. This means:

- More accurate information retrieval: LLMs can understand the true meaning behind your search queries, delivering more relevant and helpful results.
- Improved dialogue systems: Chatbots and virtual assistants will become more engaging and natural, understanding the flow of conversation and responding accordingly.

- Personalized experiences: LLMs can tailor their outputs to your specific needs and preferences, creating a more individualized and meaningful user experience.

4. Personalization Powerhouse: Imagine an LLM that tailors its outputs to your unique preferences, learning from your interactions and evolving alongside you. This raises exciting possibilities, but also necessitates careful consideration of:

- Privacy concerns: How will user data be collected and used to personalize LLM outputs? Transparency and user control are crucial.
- Bias and fairness: Personalized LLMs must be designed to avoid amplifying existing biases and ensure fair treatment for all users.
- Explainability and control: Users need to understand how personalization works and have control over their data and the LLM's outputs.

These are just a glimpse into the exciting future of LLMs. As these trends continue to develop, the potential impact on communication, creativity, and problem-solving is truly transformative. Stay tuned for the next section, where we explore the exciting career paths and skillsets for LLM developers!

The LLM landscape is buzzing with innovation, and keeping up with the latest trends can feel like chasing a runaway code snippet. Let's dissect some key advancements and their potential impact, illustrated with examples and code:

1. Multilingual Mastery: Imagine translating between languages as effortlessly as switching tabs in your browser. This future is closer than you think!

- Example: Google AI's PaLM achieved state-of-the-art results on multilingual benchmarks, translating between 54 languages with impressive fluency.
- Code (Simplified):

Python

```
# Load a multilingual LLM like PaLM or Jurassic-1
Jumbo

from transformers import AutoModelForSeq2SeqLM,
AutoTokenizer


model_name = "google/pa lm"

tokenizer =
AutoTokenizer.from_pretrained(model_name)

model =
AutoModelForSeq2SeqLM.from_pretrained(model_name)


# Translate a sentence from English to French

english_text = "Hello, how are you?"
```

```python
french_text = tokenizer.translate(english_text,
src_lang="en", tgt_lang="fr")["sequences"][0]

print(french_text)  # Output: "Bonjour, comment
allez-vous ?"



# Explore other language pairs and translation
tasks
```

2. Embracing Multimodality: Text is just the first chapter in the LLM story. Now, they're learning to interpret and generate across different mediums:

- Example: OpenAI's VQ-VAE model can generate photorealistic images based on text descriptions. Imagine describing your dream vacation destination and seeing it come to life!
- Code (Simplified):

Python

```python
# Use a library like OpenAI's API to access
VQ-VAE or similar models

import openai
```

```python
openai.api_key = "YOUR_API_KEY"


# Describe your dream vacation destination

text_description = "A secluded beach with
turquoise water and white sand, surrounded by
lush palm trees."



# Generate the image

response = openai.Image.create(

    prompt=text_description,

    n=1,

    size="512x512",

)

image_url = response["data"][0]["url"]

print(image_url)  # Access and display the
generated image
```

3. Contextual Comprehension: LLMs are no longer keyword-chasing robots. They're grasping the deeper meaning of language, making their responses more relevant:

- Example: LaMDA, a factual language model from Google AI, can engage in nuanced conversations, understanding the context and intent behind your questions.
- Code (Simplified):

Python

```
# Interact with LaMDA through Google AI's Bard
interface

# (Disclaimer: Bard is still under development)



user_query = "What are the ethical implications
of artificial intelligence?"

bard_response = bard.interact(query=user_query)

print(bard_response)  # Bard provides a
thoughtful and informative response



# Explore different conversation topics and see
how LaMDA adapts its responses
```

4. Personalization Powerhouse: Imagine an LLM that remembers your preferences and tailors its outputs to your unique needs. This has exciting potential, but also raises questions:

- Example: Netflix uses LLMs to personalize movie recommendations based on your viewing history and genre preferences.
- Code (Simplified):

Python

```python
# This is a simplified example, actual Netflix
recommendation systems are much more complex



# Simulate personalized recommendations based on
user data

user_data = {"genres": ["Sci-Fi", "Comedy"],
"recent_watches": ["Star Wars", "The Office"]}



def recommend_movie(user_data):

    # Access a database of movies and ratings

    # Consider user data and recommend similar or
related movies

    recommended_movie = "Back to the Future"
```

```
    return recommended_movie


recommended_movie = recommend_movie(user_data)

print(f"Recommended movie for you:
{recommended_movie}")
```

Remember, these are just starting points. As LLMs evolve, the possibilities are endless. But ethical considerations and responsible development are crucial to ensure this technology benefits all.

Stay tuned for the next section, where we delve into the exciting world of LLM development and the skillsets you need to be a part of this cutting-edge field!

•

9.2 LLM Developer: Dream Job or Sci-Fi Fantasy? The Reality is Even Better!

Imagine a career where you push the boundaries of language, solve real-world problems, and contribute to cutting-edge technology. Sounds like science fiction, right? Well, for LLM developers, it's the exciting reality!

The demand for skilled LLM developers is skyrocketing across various industries, making it a highly sought-after and rewarding career path. If you're passionate about language, technology, and innovation, this might be your dream job!

Why become an LLM developer?

- Be a Language Pioneer: Play a pivotal role in shaping the future of communication and AI, pushing the limits of what LLMs can do.
- Solve Real-World Problems: Apply your skills to tackle challenges in healthcare, education, finance, and more, making a positive impact on society.
- Be at the Forefront of Innovation: Work with cutting-edge technologies, collaborate with brilliant minds, and constantly learn and evolve in a dynamic field.
- High Demand & Great Opportunities: Enjoy excellent job prospects, competitive salaries, and the chance to work on groundbreaking projects.

What skills do you need?

- Coding Prowess: Proficiency in languages like Python or Java is essential for building and interacting with LLMs.
- Machine Learning Magic: Brush up on your deep learning, NLP, and AI fundamentals to understand how LLMs work and train them effectively.
- Data wrangling Wizardry: Master the art of data cleaning, preparation, and analysis, as data is the fuel for LLM development.
- Problem-Solving Gumption: Think creatively, troubleshoot challenges, and approach problems with an innovative mindset.

- Communication & Teamwork: Collaborate effectively with diverse teams, from engineers and linguists to data scientists and product managers.

How to get started?

- Online Resources: Dive into online courses, tutorials, and communities like TensorFlow, Hugging Face, and OpenAI to learn the latest advancements.
- Open-Source Projects: Contribute to open-source LLM projects like transformers or fairseq to gain hands-on experience and collaborate with other developers.
- Personal Projects: Experiment with building your own LLM for a specific task or domain, showcasing your skills and creativity.
- Stay Curious & Keep Learning: The LLM landscape is constantly evolving, so stay updated with new research, attend conferences, and network with other experts.

Remember, the journey to becoming an LLM developer is as exciting as the destination itself. Embrace the challenge, fuel your passion for language and technology, and you'll be well on your way to contributing to the future of this revolutionary field.

Ready to join the LLM revolution? The opportunities are endless! In the next chapter, we'll delve into the ethical considerations and societal implications of LLMs, ensuring we steer this powerful technology towards a positive impact.

Forget flying cars, LLM developers are shaping the future of language and AI right now! It's not just a dream job, it's a chance to be at the forefront of innovation with real-world impact. But before you start writing your sci-fi resume, let's explore the skills and resources you need to become an LLM rockstar:

1. Coding Prowess: Your Superpower

Think of code as your wand in this magical world. Python and Java are common languages, but familiarity with libraries like:

- TensorFlow: Open-source framework for building and training machine learning models, including LLMs.
- PyTorch: Another popular deep learning library offering flexibility and ease of use.
- Hugging Face Transformers: Pre-trained LLM models and tools for fine-tuning and experimentation.

Example (Simple TensorFlow code for sentiment analysis LLM):

Python

```
from tensorflow.keras.preprocessing.text import Tokenizer

from tensorflow.keras.models import Sequential

from tensorflow.keras.layers import Embedding, LSTM, Dense



# Load data and tokenize text

tokenizer = Tokenizer(num_words=10000)

tokenizer.fit_on_texts(data["text"])
```

```python
sequences =
tokenizer.texts_to_sequences(data["text"])


# Build and train the LLM model

model = Sequential()

model.add(Embedding(10000, 128,
input_length=max_length))

model.add(LSTM(64))

model.add(Dense(1, activation="sigmoid"))

model.compile(loss="binary_crossentropy",
optimizer="adam", metrics=["accuracy"])

model.fit(sequences, data["labels"], epochs=10)
```

2. Machine Learning Magic: Unveiling the Secrets

Deep learning, NLP, and AI are the building blocks of LLMs.
Understanding how they work is crucial:

- Deep learning: Algorithms learn from data, and LLMs are
  trained on massive amounts of text and code.
- Natural Language Processing (NLP): Techniques for
  computers to understand and process human language.
- AI fundamentals: Explore concepts like machine learning
  algorithms, neural networks, and optimization techniques.

Example (Exploring pre-trained LLMs with Hugging Face Transformers):

Python

```python
from transformers import AutoTokenizer,
AutoModelForSequenceClassification


# Load a pre-trained sentiment analysis LLM

tokenizer =
AutoTokenizer.from_pretrained("bert-base-uncased"
)

model =
AutoModelForSequenceClassification.from_pretraine
d("bert-base-uncased")


# Analyze sentiment of a sentence

text = "This movie was amazing!"

encoded_text = tokenizer(text,
return_tensors="pt")

output = model(**encoded_text)

prediction = output[0].argmax().item()
```

```python
if prediction == 0:

  print("Negative sentiment")

else:

  print("Positive sentiment")
```

3. Data Wrangling Wizardry: The Unsung Hero

LLMs are data hungry! Mastering data cleaning, preparation, and analysis is essential:

- Data cleaning: Remove noise, inconsistencies, and errors from your training data.
- Data preparation: Feature engineering, tokenization, and formatting data for the LLM.
- Data analysis: Analyze model performance, identify biases, and improve training data quality.

Example (Data cleaning with Pandas for LLM training):

Python

```python
import pandas as pd


# Load and clean your LLM training data

data = pd.read_csv("movie_reviews.csv")
```

```python
data.dropna(subset=["text", "label"],
inplace=True)

data["text"] = data["text"].str.lower()   #
Lowercase for consistency


# Split data into training, validation, and test
sets

from sklearn.model_selection import
train_test_split


X_train, X_val, y_train, y_val =
train_test_split(data["text"], data["label"],
test_size=0.2)
```

Remember, the journey is just as exciting as the destination. Embrace online courses, contribute to open-source projects like TensorFlow Hub or Hugging Face models, and stay curious! The future of LLMs is yours to shape, one line of code at a time.

In the next chapter, we'll explore the ethical considerations and societal implications of LLMs, ensuring this powerful technology benefits all. Join us as we navigate the responsible development of this revolutionary field!

9.3 Stay Ahead of the Curve: Your Guide to LLM Mastery in a Fast-Paced World

The world of LLMs is like a fast-flowing river – exciting, transformative, but demanding constant adaptation. So, how do you stay afloat and become an LLM master, navigating the ever-evolving currents? Buckle up, because we're diving into your essential survival kit:

1. Become a Lifelong Learner:

- Online Resources: Dive deep into online courses, tutorials, and communities like:
    - TensorFlow
    - Hugging Face
    - OpenAI
    - Coursera, edX, Udacity (for structured learning)
-
- Stay Updated: Follow blogs, newsletters, and attend conferences like:
    - NeurIPS, ACL, EMNLP
    - Industry-specific events relevant to your domain (e.g., healthcare, finance)
-
- Embrace Experimentation: Don't be afraid to get your hands dirty with personal projects. Try:
    - Fine-tuning pre-trained LLMs for specific tasks
    - Building your own LLM for a niche domain
    - Experimenting with different LLM architectures
-

2. Open-Source Collaboration: The Power of Together

- Contribute to Open-Source Projects:
    - TensorFlow Hub, Hugging Face Transformers
    - Fairseq, OpenAI Universe
-
- Connect with the Community:
    - Participate in online forums, discussions, and hackathons
    - Find mentors and collaborators with shared interests
-

3. Industry Events & Conferences: Network and Get Inspired

- Attend industry events and conferences to:
    - Learn about the latest research and advancements
    - Network with experts, potential employers, and collaborators
    - Discover new applications and challenges in your field
-

Remember:

- Continuous Learning is Key: The LLM landscape is ever-changing, so embrace the growth mindset and stay curious.
- Specialization is Valuable: While a strong foundation is crucial, consider specializing in a specific domain (e.g., healthcare, finance) to stand out.
- Ethics & Responsibility Matter: As LLMs become more powerful, understanding and advocating for ethical development is essential.

By following these tips and staying passionate, you'll be well on your way to LLM mastery, shaping the future of this revolutionary technology for good.

Ready to explore the ethical considerations and societal implications of LLMs? In the next chapter, we'll delve into the crucial questions surrounding responsible AI development, ensuring this powerful tool benefits all.

The LLM landscape is a thrilling rapids ride – exhilarating, unpredictable, and demanding constant adaptation. But fear not, language adventurer! With the right tools and mindset, you can navigate the ever-evolving currents and become an LLM master. Here's your essential survival kit, complete with examples and code to jumpstart your journey:

1. Become a Lifelong Learner:

- Online Resources: Dive deep with these:
  - Interactive Courses:
    - Coursera: "Natural Language Processing with Deep Learning" specialization by deeplearning.ai
    - edX: "Introduction to TensorFlow for Artificial Intelligence" by Google AI
    - Udacity: "Intro to Natural Language Processing Nanodegree" by Udacity
  -
  - Community Hubs:
    - **TensorFlow:**Tutorials, guides, and community forums (https://www.tensorflow.org/)

- - Hugging Face: Open-source library, datasets, and courses (https://huggingface.co/)
    - OpenAI: Research papers, blog posts, and access to their GPT-3 language model (https://openai.com/)
  -
  - Industry-Specific Events:
    - Healthcare: AMIA Conference, HIMSS
    - Finance: Quant Summit, AI in Finance Forum
  -
-
- Embrace Experimentation: Get your hands dirty with personal projects:
- Fine-tuning Pre-trained LLMs:

  * Use Hugging Face Transformers to fine-tune a pre-trained LLM like BERT for sentiment analysis:

```python
from transformers import AutoTokenizer, AutoModelForSequenceClassification

tokenizer = AutoTokenizer.from_pretrained("bert-base-uncased")
model = AutoModelForSequenceClassification.from_pretrained("bert-base-uncased")

# Train the model on your sentiment-labeled dataset
```

```python
# Use the fine-tuned model for sentiment
analysis
text = "This movie was amazing!"
encoded_text = tokenizer(text,
return_tensors="pt")
output = model(**encoded_text)
prediction = output[0].argmax().item()

if prediction == 0:
    print("Negative sentiment")
else:
    print("Positive sentiment")
```

-
- Building Your Own LLM:

 * Explore libraries like OpenAI Gym or DeepMind
Lab to create custom environments for training
your LLM on specific tasks.

-
- Exploring Architectures:

 * Compare and experiment with different LLM
architectures like transformers and recurrent
neural networks using online tutorials and code
repositories.

-
-

2. Open-Source Collaboration: The Power of Together

- Contribute to Open-Source Projects:
    - TensorFlow Hub: Share your machine learning models with the community (https://tfhub.dev/)
    - Hugging Face Transformers: Contribute to the library's development or create your own language models and datasets (https://huggingface.co/)
    - Fairseq: Help develop high-performance sequence modeling tools (<invalid URL removed>)
-
- Connect with the Community:
    - Online Forums: Actively participate in discussions on platforms like Reddit's r/MachineLearning or Hugging Face's community forum.
    - Hackathons: Join events like TensorFlow Hackathons or Kaggle competitions to collaborate and solve real-world challenges.
    - Finding Mentors & Collaborators: Connect with experienced individuals on platforms like LinkedIn or attend meetups organized by local AI groups.
-

3. Industry Events & Conferences:

- Expand Your Horizons: Attend industry events like:
    - NeurIPS: The Neural Information Processing Systems conference showcases cutting-edge research in AI and machine learning.
    - ACL: The Annual Meeting of the Association for Computational Linguistics focuses on advancements in computational linguistics and NLP.

- ○ EMNLP: The Empirical Methods in Natural Language Processing conference presents research on the empirical evaluation of NLP methods.

-

Remember:

- Continuous Learning is Key: Stay updated with the latest advancements through online resources, conferences, and personal projects.
- Specialization is Valuable: Consider focusing on a specific domain to deepen your expertise and stand out in the job market.
- Ethics & Responsibility Matter: Advocate for the ethical development and responsible use of LLMs to ensure they benefit society as a whole.

By embracing these tips and actively engaging with the LLM community, you'll be well on your way to becoming an LLM master, shaping the future of this powerful technology for good. Remember, the journey is just as exciting as the destination, so enjoy the ride!

Chapter 10: Conquering the LLM Frontier - Where Do We Go From Here?

Whoa, hold your metaphorical horses, intrepid language adventurer! Before you charge off to build the next game-changing LLM application, let's take a moment to bask in the glory of all we've achieved. Buckle up, because we're about to recap the key takeaways, explore where to fuel your LLM fire further, and even tease some ideas for building your own groundbreaking applications.

- ## 10.1: Knowledge Nuggets - Your Personalized Treasure Chest of LLM Gems
- Congratulations! You've embarked on an incredible journey through the fascinating world of LLMs. As you take a moment to reflect, here are the key takeaways you can hold onto as valuable gems in your personal treasure chest of knowledge:
- 1. LLMs: The Language Leaders of Tomorrow: Forget fancy chatbots - LLMs are poised to revolutionize how we communicate, create, and solve problems across diverse fields. They're not just the future of language, they're shaping the future of our world!
- 2. The Learning Curve: A Thrilling Ascent, Not a Terrifying Climb: While the realm of LLMs might seem complex, with the right resources and a touch of determination, anyone can become an LLM whiz. Remember, the journey is filled with exciting discoveries and a supportive community to guide you.
- 3. The Community: Your Secret Weapon in the LLM Quest: The LLM community is your powerhouse of support and

inspiration. From open-source projects where you can collaborate with like-minded individuals to engaging forums and events, you'll find a wealth of knowledge and encouragement to fuel your LLM journey.

- 4. Ethics: The Guiding Compass for Responsible LLMs: As LLMs evolve, it's crucial to remember the importance of ethical development. By prioritizing responsible practices, we can ensure that these powerful language models benefit everyone and contribute to a positive future.
- Remember, these gems of knowledge are just the beginning. Keep exploring, keep learning, and keep contributing to the LLM revolution. The future is unwritten, and you have the power to help shape it with the incredible potential of LLMs!

1. LLMs: The Language Leaders of Tomorrow:

- Imagine an LLM that can translate between hundreds of languages flawlessly, breaking down communication barriers and fostering global understanding.
- Consider an LLM that can write different kinds of creative content, from poems and code to scripts and musical pieces, democratizing creative expression.
- Envision an LLM that can analyze vast amounts of data and generate personalized insights, transforming fields like healthcare and education.

2. The Learning Curve: A Thrilling Ascent, Not a Terrifying Climb:

- Start with beginner-friendly online courses or tutorials on platforms like Coursera or edX.
- Participate in online communities like Hugging Face or TensorFlow forums to ask questions and learn from others.
- Begin with simple LLM tasks like sentiment analysis or text summarization to build your confidence and skills.

3. The Community: Your Secret Weapon in the LLM Quest:

- Contribute to open-source LLM projects like TensorFlow Hub or Hugging Face Transformers to make a real impact and learn from others.
- Attend meetups or conferences related to LLMs to network with experts and fellow enthusiasts.
- Follow prominent researchers and practitioners in the field on social media or blogs to stay updated on the latest advancements.

4. Ethics: The Guiding Compass for Responsible LLMs:

- Be aware of potential biases in LLM training data and algorithms, and advocate for fair and inclusive development practices.
- Consider the societal implications of LLMs, such as job displacement or the spread of misinformation, and promote responsible use.
- Stay informed about ethical guidelines and regulations surrounding LLMs, and contribute to discussions about their responsible development.

By incorporating these examples and continuing your exploration of LLMs, you can turn your treasure chest of knowledge into a springboard for exciting future endeavors!

10.2: Where to Find Your Next LLM Fix – A Buffet of Resources to Keep You Hooked

Feeling that post-chapter lull but still craving more LLM goodness? Don't worry, language adventurer, the learning never ends! We've compiled a delectable spread of resources to satisfy your hunger for knowledge and keep you fueled on your LLM journey:

For the Structured Learner:

- Online Courses: Dive deep with platforms like Coursera, edX, and Udacity. They offer structured learning paths, from beginner-friendly introductions to advanced specialization courses, taught by industry experts. Explore courses like "Natural Language Processing with Deep Learning" on Coursera or "Introduction to TensorFlow for Artificial Intelligence" on edX.
- Community Hubs: Immerse yourself in the vibrant LLM communities around TensorFlow, Hugging Face, and OpenAI. These hubs provide comprehensive tutorials, forums filled with passionate discussions, and the latest advancements fresh from the researchers themselves. Get hands-on with tutorials on TensorFlow Hub or explore the diverse datasets and pre-trained models available on Hugging Face.

For the Networking Enthusiast:

- Industry-Specific Events: Expand your horizons and connect with professionals in your field at industry-specific events like NeurIPS for general AI research, ACL for computational linguistics, or EMNLP for empirical methods in NLP. These events offer presentations, workshops, and poster sessions, providing valuable insights and networking opportunities.

- Hackathons & Meetups: Put your skills to the test and collaborate with other LLM enthusiasts at exciting hackathons like TensorFlow Hackathons or Kaggle competitions. You can also find local meetups organized by groups like AI for Good or Women in Machine Learning to connect with like-minded individuals and discuss the latest trends.

For the Self-Directed Devourer:

- Books & Articles: Stay ahead of the curve by delving into the latest research papers, blog posts, and books by renowned authors in the field. Explore blogs like The Gradient by Google AI or publications like arXiv to stay updated on cutting-edge research. Immerse yourself in books like "Deep Learning with Python" by Francois Chollet or "Speech and Language Processing" by Dan Jurafsky and James H. Martin for in-depth knowledge.

Remember, this is just a starting point! The LLM landscape is constantly evolving, so embrace the spirit of exploration and keep seeking out new resources to fuel your passion. With dedication and the right tools, you can keep expanding your LLM expertise and become a true master of this revolutionary technology.

P.S. Feeling overwhelmed by the buffet? Don't be afraid to start small and pick resources that align with your interests and goals. The key is to be consistent and enjoy the learning process!

10.3: Your Creative Playground – Building Innovative LLM Applications

Ready to unleash the power of LLMs and turn your ideas into reality? Buckle up, innovator, because this is where the magic happens! Here's your launchpad to explore exciting possibilities and build groundbreaking applications:

Remember:

- LLMs are powerful tools, but ethics matter. Always prioritize responsible development and consider the potential impact of your application.
- Start small, experiment, and iterate. Don't be afraid to begin with simple projects and gradually scale up as you gain experience.
- The LLM community is your support system. Collaborate, share your ideas, and learn from others on your journey.

Now, let your imagination soar! Here are just a few sparks to ignite your creativity:

For the Educator:

- Personalized learning companion: Craft an LLM-powered tutor that adapts to individual learning styles and paces, making education more engaging and effective.
- Interactive storytelling: Design an LLM-driven storytelling platform that generates personalized narratives based on user preferences, fostering creativity and language skills.

- Automatic feedback and assessment: Develop an LLM that provides real-time feedback on writing assignments, identifying areas for improvement and offering suggestions.

For the Creator:

- AI-powered music composition: Train an LLM to generate music based on emotions, genres, or even specific instruments, democratizing music creation.
- Next-level content generation: Design an LLM that writes different creative text formats, like poems, code, scripts, or even personalized marketing copy, tailored to your audience.
- Interactive fiction and games: Build immersive experiences with LLMs that respond to user choices and actions, blurring the lines between reality and imagination.

For the Problem Solver:

- Intelligent customer service: Develop an LLM-powered chatbot that understands user intent and provides exceptional support, revolutionizing customer service experiences.
- Automated medical diagnosis: Train an LLM to analyze medical data and provide insights to healthcare professionals, potentially aiding in early diagnosis and treatment.
- Personalized language translation: Create an LLM that goes beyond simple translation, capturing nuances and cultural contexts for seamless communication across languages.

Remember, these are just starting points. The possibilities are truly endless!

Ready to take the leap? Here are some resources to empower you:

- Open-source LLM projects: Contribute to projects like TensorFlow Hub or Hugging Face Transformers to gain experience and collaborate with others.
- Hackathons and challenges: Participate in events like Kaggle competitions or LLM-focused hackathons to test your skills and build innovative solutions.
- Online communities: Engage with the LLM community on platforms like Reddit's r/MachineLearning or Hugging Face's forum to learn, share ideas, and find inspiration.

So, what are you waiting for? Dive into the world of LLM development, unleash your creativity, and build applications that make a positive impact on the world. The future is waiting, and you have the power to shape it with the power of language!

www.ingramcontent.com/pod-product-compliance
Lightning Source LLC
LaVergne TN
LVHW051737050326
832903LV00023B/958